COMMUNAL SOCIETIES IN AMERICA
AN AMS REPRINT SERIES

Communities
of the
Past And
Present

Published by L ano Colonist
Newllano, Louisiana
1924

Composition, printing and binding by
Llano Co-operative Colony

AMS PRESS
NEW YORK

Library of Congress Cataloging in Publication Data

.Wooster, Ernest S.
  Communities of the past and present.

  (Communal societies in America)
  Reprint of the 1924 ed. published by Llano Colonist,
Newllano, La.
    1. Collective settlements—United States—History.
I. Title.
HX653.W6 1974   335'.9'73   72–2946
  ISBN 0-404-10712-5

Reprinted from the edition of 1924, Newllano, La.
First AMS edition published in 1974
Manufactured in the United States of America

AMS PRESS INC.
NEW YORK, N.Y. 10003

CONTENTS

INTRODUCTION

By Job Harriman

*Founder of Llano del Rio Co-operative Colony and for
Ten Years Its President*

After twenty-four years of activity in the Socialist movement, I came to the conclusion that we
should have to add economic activities to our political activities, or we should never succeed. It became apparent to me that a people would never
abandon their means of livelihood, good or bad,
capitalistic or otherwise, until other methods were
developed which would promise advantages at least
as good as those by which they were living.

It was and still is my opinion that all laws providing for economic changes must be preceded by
industrial development that gives rise to such laws
And propaganda prior to such industrial development must fail, whether such propaganda proposes
to work out changes by parliamentary action or by
an armed revolution.

Having this thought in view and having been
trained in the Marxian school of economics, I proceeded to organize the colony in line with that philosophy.

The American branch of that school had unduly
stressed the theory of economic determinism as well
as the materialistic and mechanistic theory of life.
Believing in the doctrines so stressed, persons holding the same views were naturally sought, until a
sufficient number were found with whom to form
the board of directors of the Llano del Rio Company.

Believing that life arose out of chemical action and that form was determined by the impinging environment, I naturally concluded that all would react more or less alike to the same environment and for that reason laid down the principles of equal wage, equal educational and social advantages, and equal comforts, including housing and commissary furnishings.

Having gained the assent of the Board and got the details worked out, we proceeded to sell stock and locate the members on the ground. While we were surprised at the different attitudes of the new-comers toward the entire institution as well as toward its various departments and toward each other, yet we consoled ourselves with the rationalization that it was all due to the difference between a co-operative institution and the institutions with which they were accustomed to deal.

As time passed our interest increased, especially in the facts observed.

The reactions were not at all in line with what we had expected.

Men and women would gather around the fire in the large hotel room of an evening and discuss the various phases of socialism as they had imagined them; and if a stranger were present they would present substantially the same views and the same arguments in more or less the same form according to the accepted doctrine of socialism. And yet these very same people when in the shop or field would act as differently as they would have acted had they never heard of socialism.

Some were selfish, arrogant, and egotistical and shirked their duties, quit early, went to work late, rested often, talked much, criticized everything and everybody, wanted the lion's share at the commissary, wanted the best houses, with extra furniture, neglected the animals, were careless with tools, and did everything that might be thought of by those who were seeking the advantage of those about them.

This behavior was a bold attack upon our theories. We had imagined that men who believed in socialism would react more or less alike to the same environment, but when we saw that they persisted in their so-called reactions, I, at least, became convinced that theories or intellectual concepts play a very small part in our reactions.

Another fact that struck at the very foundation of our theory was that the line between the selfish and the unselfish was not drawn between the classes according to our philosophy. Economic determinism seemed to play no part in separating the sheep from the goats.

We had a number of men who were well-to-do, with good homes outside and money in the bank, and many of course who had put in their last dollar.

We found more well-to-do men among the unselfish than there were among the selfish, as manifested by their behavior. When the accounts of the unselfish, both rich and poor, were examined, they showed that the unselfish well-to-do had drawn less from the commissary than they had been accustomed to living upon, and less than others who had not been accustomed to as much as they were than drawing. This class of unselfish people were working out an idea and were willing to live upon as little as possible while it was being done. The unselfish well-to-do were willing to, and did, lend money to the colony, but they would not accept more than their pro-rata of what the colony could afford, always saying, "We are willing to do what we expect others to do."

On the other hand, there were selfish people, both among the rich and the poor, who drew everything they could get from the commissary, and, as stated above, conducted themselves likewise in regard to every other department of the colony and in respect to the service they rendered. We found to our surprise that there were more selfish men among the poor, in proportion to their number, than there were among the well-to-do.

The line of selfishness and unselfishness was not drawn, as we expected it would be, between the rich and the poor; nor was it drawn in the place we expected within each of these classes. The majority was on the wrong side of the line; that is, the majority of the well-to-do were on the unselfish side, and the reverse was true with the poor. Worst of all and most unexpected was the fact that the selfish persisted in their course with a persistence that was amazing.

We came to see that the philosophy of socialism played a very small part in their behavior and that time did not alter this course very much.

After three years' observation, some of us were convinced that the materialistic philosophy, including economic determinism, was not sufficient to explain the phenomena that were going on about us. It was apparent that human beings were not mere chemical compounds, however complex, that were mentally and otherwise reacting to whatever environment; but in addition to such environment and reaction, there is a potential energy that is acting of its own accord; that is, indeed, the driving force not only in man, but in all living things.

The fact that all held the same philosophy and yet behaved so very differently, some even to the positive detriment of the colony, forced upon us, as much as any other one thing, the conclusion that behavior is not determined by our philosophy, nor yet by any idea that we may entertain, but that it is determined by the quality of one's emotions and feelings which motive one's ideas or philosophy.

Having arrived at this conclusion, it became extremely important that we should ascertain how it is that the emotions or feelings motive the ideas.

It appears from what we have observed that mental development may proceed to a high degree and yet continue to be a manifestation of selfishness, greed, ambition, and every phase of the passions. On the other hand, it appears that a high quality of emotional, ethical, or spiritual development may be attained with either a moderate or high degree of mental development. The conclusion finally reached is that the intellect is only a manifestation of certain states of feeling. If those feelings be of the passions, then as a matter of course the mind or intellect will be a manifestation of those passions; that is to say, the intellect will be motived by those feelings. On the other hand, if the feelings have undergone a long period of ethical or spiritual training, it follows that the intellect will be a manifestation of such training; that is to say, it will be motived by such ethical feelings.

We accordingly found that the problems arising within a colony were exceedingly complex; that men cannot be classified according to the opinions they express; that the opinions are only indications, but may be altogether unreliable, as in the case of the socialist theory and the behavior of the devotees; that mental and ethical tests must be made part of the questionnaire and then a period of probation be required, during which time the real state of feelings of the applicant may be ascertained; that is to say, whether he is governed by his passions or by his ethical and spiritual feelings.

It is plain that the training of children must be conducted in such manner as to induce the unfoldment of the ethical and spiritual nature. Failure so to do means the destruction of the Community itself. However important the spiritual quality may be, yet it is imperative that the child's mind must be free from the influence of dogmas and kept in a receptive and scientific attitude, else the result will be a devotee to some set or system of formulas, when mental and spiritual growth stops while endless repetition goes on.

In a community where the economic interests are common, ethical and psychological problems play a far more important part, are far more difficult to handle, and are, accordingly, more far-reaching in their consequences than under other circumstances.

Where each owns his own property and is struggling to increase his holdings, the mind is largely centered upon methods of production and commercial transactions and is only slightly occupied with social relations, such being of minor importance in so far as the purpose of accumulating property is involved. Besides, if he does not approve of the conduct of his neighbor, he may withdraw and exclude this neighbor from his thought and life.

In a Community, however, an entirely different state of affairs exists. The mind of the individual is only slightly concerned with commercial transactions, and then not with the deal itself, but only with final results. This removes from the minds of the colonists the necessity of considering how to take advantage in a trade, which is so often present in commercial transactions and which becomes the rock upon which the morale of many is wrecked. The mind is accordingly freer to entertain the problems of production with a more scientific attitude. The problem, however, does not stop here. There is a tendency to shift this responsibility and to leave it to others. This tendency finds its full expression in those dominated by the passions, while those of a highly developed ethical sense are always found at their posts.

At this point there is a kind of behavior that appears and, unless understood, becomes very confusing. There will be found those who are extremely active and yet who are also extremely selfish. If their behavior is closely observed, they will be invariably found to be working for self-glory, for power, or for some advantage which, if defeated, will end their activities; while the reverse is true with the highly spiritual person.

The ethical and spiritual quality, therefore, becomes of primary importance in community life. They are the very foundation upon which a Community must be built if stability and durability are to be attained. It must not be forgotten, however, that a scientific attitude of mind is likewise equally important, else the growth and unfoldment of the individual will be paralized by dogmas and the Community will sink into a sordid struggle for gain and physical comforts which will in turn undermine the morale of the community.

Returning to the thought that under a system of private ownership of property one may exclude from his thought and companionship whomsoever he may dislike, we wish to point out that in a co-operative community this cannot be done. On the contrary, in a community one is compelled to modify his views,

to change his hostile attitudes, and to adjust himself
to his neighbor, to whom he is bound both by economic and social ties—the economic factor being almost, if not quite, eliminated.

In this fact is found a powerful stimulant to ethical growth and to genuine spiritual unfoldment. The
process is continuous, ofttimes straining even to the
breaking point, but always upbuilding if the adjustment is made. The process admits of individual development, for it is the individual who succeeds in
making the adjustment that grows even though his
adversary fails in his adjustment and goes down in
the struggle.

Though the process is constantly going on, most
people are unconscious of the results and seem to
remain thus unconscious until for some reason they
depart from the colony. It is then, and not until
then, that they begin to appreciate the advantages
of community life, though many cannot explain the
reasons. They find themselves longing to return, especially those who had succeeded in adjusting themselves to others. It is out of such adjustment that often spring the finest friendships and the most delightful relations of life.

Another evidence of real growth caused by
such experiences is that those who have been successful colonists, in the above sense, become more
successful in the affairs of life than they ever were
before their colony experience; nevertheless, there
is in such persons an ever-increasing desire to return.

This seems at least to indicate that the close
relationships sustained in community life more nearly conform to our fundamental gregarious urge than
does the system of individual ownership of property.
It seems to break the economic shackles that otherwise find the feelings and emotions and yet at the
same time impose upon them the responsibility of
self-control which is, after all, the essence of character formation.

It will be observed from the foregoing that such
a community as has been described becomes a living organism. That there are certain moral, ethical,
and spiritual qualities for which there are definite,

ascertainable reasons, and which may, if understood, continuously grow and unfold, conditioned always upon the fact that the attitude of mind be always scientific and not at all dogmatic.

Nor must it be forgotten that the scientific mind may become the most dogmatic of all because of a belief in some fact which seems to be demonstrated. Only the highest quality and most tender and kindly feelings for the welfare of others can prevent this dogmatic attitude. The moment an idea becomes more important than the welfare of the humblest being, that moment the individual who entertains the idea enters upon the dogmatic highway.

Whoever thoughtfully lives in a community and adjusts himself to its life and growing needs, must learn that at best any theory or viewpoint or supposed fact can serve only as working hypothesis, a point from which to start for a new goal. This is the chief element in, and the secret of, growth.

ADDENDA

Since the printing of the first sections of this book, much additional matter has come to the writer. Mr. John Duss of Old Economy, the last home of the Rappites, sends in some valuable matter.

Lincoln Phifer sends the writer a brief summary of the Nevada Colony at Fallon. Mr. Phifer was associated with the colony for a short time, and as a newspaper man and trained observer, his account deserves space which it was impossible to grant it in this volume, as the section devoted to the account of the Nevada Colony had already gone to press.

Mr. Duss's letter is of special interest, for it shows that the Harmonites have not always been truthfully and considerately handled by those who have essayed to report them. For fear that the author of this little volume may appear in a like light, we hasten to offer such apologies as may be required for the account herein given, and only regret that the material sent by Mr. Duss was not available before the first section, containing the account of the Harmonites, had gone to press. However, we reprint a portion of his letter, and hope in the next edition to make amends for any transgressions that may appear here. Mr. Duss writes, on July 8, 1924:

"Ernest S. Wooster: Am just back from the hospital, where I was taken * * * I am out of patience with historians in general as to what they write in regard to the Harmony Society. Some of Hinds' matter is good, but as I recollect it is not what it should be toward the end. Have not looked at what he has to say for 20 years, so my mind is not quite clear as to the subject * * * You will note that we had a Centennial (of the Harmony Society) here last month. I gave every month of the six months prior to June 6 to the preparation for it, and it was probably due to this over-exertion that I was stricken down. However, I have the satisfaction that all sides proclaim the celebration as the most wonderful thing of the sort that ever was seen anywhere."

ERROR—Page 90. The title "Bo any Bay Mutineers" should be "Bounty Mutineers."

Communities
of the Past

THE EPHRATA COMMUNITY

1728—1900

Important chiefly because it shows the longevity possible to co-operative Communities, the Ephrata Community deserves first mention, as being one of the earliest formed and also one which endured through several generations.

Conrad Beissel (also known as Beisel and Peysel) after living as a recluse for several years, was convinced that the seventh day of the week should be observed as a day of worship. In 1728 he published a work on this subject which gave him a small following. Three men and two women shared his wilderness seclusion with him. They formed the nucleus for a community which at one time had 300 inhabitants, and owned much property, including some enormous dwellings. A paper mill, flour mill, oil mill, fulling mill, bakery, printery, school house, and other small buildings, with much land, made up the property of this group. Governor Penn, who frequently visited the Beissel Colony, offered them a tract of 5000 acres, but the offer was declined on the grounds that it might be injurious to the spiritual life of the community to accumulate much property.

All the members stood on perfect equality. They had no written agreement, but followed the New Testament. All property was held in common, but no member was obliged to surrender any of his own individual possessions. The source of income was farming and manufacturing. As late as 1900 this community was still in existence; but it was small in membership and no longer vigorous.

Ephrata, as it became known, was a celibate community, though no vows on celibacy were taken, and marriage was allowed. Mr. Hinds comments on Ephrata as follows:

"While Ephrata may excite an interest because of its common property, common labor, equality of conditions for all its members, their sincerity, simplicity, and godliness, and its unparalled longevity, having existed for 175 years, there is in its life, history, and achievements little worthy of the name of "Community."

The material success was undoubtedly great, but there was a sacrifice of intellectual attainments, social life, and all that most people consider essential to happiness. The Ephrata Colony's 175 years show the length of life possible to this sort of society.

1

THE HARMONISTS
1804—1900

Another colony which endured for more than a century, though it became less vigorous and failed to hold its young people because of the peculiarities of its beliefs, were the Harmonists, also known as Rappites. They demonstrated the material possibilities of Community living in a very convincing manner; and, while their social life may not have been all that many people would like, especially in its later history, that does not destroy the value of the evidence, and merely shows that institutions of this kind, like all others, must keep pace with the times and not become set in ruts. A certain carelessness in the business end of the enterprise indicates a loss of vigor; their celibacy, of course, doomed them to virtual extinction, as it has other colonies which have attained material and spiritual success.

George Rapp, born in 1757 in Wurtemberg, came to America in 1803 and with associates, including his son John, selected 5000 acres in Butler County, Pennsylvania. During the following year his disciples followed in three ships. All property was placed in a common fund and all agreed to labor for the good of the community, submit to its laws, and in case of withdrawal never to demand remuneration for their own labor or that of their children.

The years following their community organization were years of severe toil, hardship, and trial. The land was entirely unimproved. Nearly a shipload of their friends were induced to locate elsewhere. Others would not enter with the Colony after coming. Some of the most wealthy withdrew, taking their property. Many had complaints to make. Credit was injured by these things and the report that the society was about to break up. But the loyal ones pledged themselves to live on roots if necessary, and convinced themselves that there could be no such thing as failure. A visitor wrote of them five years later:

"We were struck with surprise and admiration at the astonishing progress in improvements and the establishment of manufactories * * * They have done more essential good for their country in five years than the same number of families scattered about the country have done in fifty. And this arises from their unity and brotherly love, added to their uniform and persevering industry. They know no mercenary views, no self-interest, except that which adds to the interest and happiness of the whole community. All are equally industrious, for an idler has no companion. If any should fall into bad practices of idleness or intoxication, he is kindly admonished by the head of the Family, backed by the countenance and wishes of all the rest; but if he is found incorrigible, he is excluded from the society; so there is no opening for the practice of vice and immorality * * * "

Another visitor wrote: "Sometimes nearly the whole force of the Society, male and female, is directed to one object, such as pulling flax, reaping, hoeing corn, etc., so that the labor of a hundred-acre field is accomplished in a day or two. * * * "

While thus prospering in this first home of their choice, the Harmonites resolved on removal, because of the unsuitableness of the soil and climate to their favorite employment—growing of grapes; for they were 12 miles from navigation, and because their acreage was inadequate to their number. In 1814 they sold nearly 6,000 acres of land, their factories, mills, shops, and village property of all kinds for the low price of $100,000 and with it purchased 30,000 acres, mostly of unimproved government land, in the Wabash Valley in Indiana. They secured rich bottoms and fertile uplands suitable for meadow and grain fields, pasture, and vineyard. They had timber and quarries and water power. They built a new town which they called Harmony, and all operations were conducted on a larger scale than before. Their commerce extended to New Orleans and their manufactures included large quantities of wollen and cotton goods; they had branch stores in different places, their number increased, and they had 1000 persons in their community. More than 150 houses were in their village, half of logs, the rest of brick or frame. Three thousand acres were brought under cultivation, and they had many vineyards.

But in this new home many of their number were afflicted with malaria; collisions occurred with their unfriendly and ignorant neighbors; some longed to return to Pennsylvania; and at the end of ten years the resolution was taken to do so if they could sell their Indiana possessions, which they succeeded in doing, though at a great sacrifice, to Robert Owen.

They began, in 1825, the building of their third colony in Beaver County, Pennsylvania, calling this town Economy. It was located on the east side of the Ohio river, about 20 miles from Pittsburg. Here again they built shops and mills, planted trees and vines, cleared land and started industries.

The Duke of Saxe-Weimar described the community in glowing terms:

"It had a thousand inhabitants. Every house was occupied, every factory fully manned. There was a fine museum; costly paintings * * ornamented the house built for the founder, and evidences of prosperity everywhere gladdened the eye. Sixty or seventy girls collected in one factory room and with their venerated leader seated in their midst sang their spiritual and other songs. With real emotion did I

4

witness this interesting scene. Their factories and workshops were warmed in winter by means of pipes connected with the steam-engine and all of the workmen had healthy complexions and moved me deeply by the warm-hearted friendliness with which they saluted the elder Rapp. I was also much gratified to see vessels containing fresh, sweet-scented flowers on all the machines. The neatness which universally reigned was in every respect worthy of praise. Huge three and four-story structures, then or soon thereafter used as woolen, cotton, and silk mills, or for other purposes, were built."

But five years later, in 1831, the great secession occurred, led by a counterfeit Count de Leon, taking 250 members and $105,000 in money. This bogus count came with a flattering letter and words of praise, announcing himself as "the Ambassador and Annointed of God, of the stem of Judah, of the root of David," and won the confidence of Rapp and others. The simple-minded and very religious Harmonists were ready for such a personage, and the "count" was received with great ceremony and rejoicing. Leon favored better clothing, better food, more personal comforts, less work, and all of the privilege of marriage. He caused a schism in the Colony, and only the kind-heartedness of the Rappites prevented the malcontents from being sent out. All of the dissenters joined with Leon and a vote was taken. Five hundred stood with Rapp, 250 went with Leon, who took $105,000 with them as the result of a compromise. Leon and his followers purchased 800 acres of land ten miles away and started a new community, which exhausted its funds within a year. The count then organized a mob of eighty persons who entered Economy for the avowed purpose of forcing additional payment from the Rappites; but neighbors rallied to the defense of the latter, and the invaders were driven off. The "count" had as one of his projects a scheme to extract gold from the rocks in his special laboratory. When he failed to do this, his followers rebelled and drove him out. He went into Louisiana and died a year later. Though this was all a severe strain on the Harmonites, it purged them of the malcontents and gave them greater peace and prosperity than ever.

In summing up the reasons why the Harmonists failed to continue this prosperity, several reasons are given by Mr. Hinds: Celibacy was adopted, and few young people joined. The tremendous personality of the elder Rapp, and to a lesser degree his adopted son, had furnished the initial energy. But with their removal by death, there was no strong central personality. With celibacy operating to prevent growth from within and to deter members from joining, the end was almost inevitable. It was not a self-perpetuating society.

The Rappites destroyed, voluntarily, all individual records of property ownership, so that it all went to the colony. After a lawsuit by a dissatisfied member, the agreement was made that all property brought in by new members must belong to the community as a whole. The Rappites gave up the use of tobacco.

Mr. Hinds says: "Probably every community that has lived long enough to accumulate any considerable property has had serious troubles with persons claiming that they were rightfully part owners thereof. Those who left a community for its good or were expelled from it because they sought to change or destroy its very life, are the ones to be first in at the death. In June, 1894, certain persons claiming to be heirs filed a bill in the U. S. Circuit Court at Pittsburg. Scandalous charges were made against various members of the society, and it was asked that the society be dissolved. However, as in cases of other communities, the rights of the colony were upheld against these sinister birds of prey."

In an earlier suit, 1821, action was brought against the Society by one Eugene Miller, who had been a member, to recover wages for labor and services rendered. The suit was rightfully decided against the complainant on the ground that in signing the articles of association he had formally renounced all claim for wages. The court held that those who secede lose all property rights separate from the colony.

In a case in 1849, brought eventually before the Supreme Court of the United States, lasting seven years in all, and enlisting such eminent counsel for the plaintiff as Edwin M. Stanton, later Secretary of War for Abraham Lincoln, a verdict was obtained for the colony, setting a precedent which will be difficult to overturn. This is known as the Nachtrieb case and seems to set at rest forever in this country the rights of individuals in such a community.

Although the Harmonites dwindled in numbers, they did some splendid things. Half a century after leaving the Indiana home, they spent several thousand dollars for the benefit of the citizens of New Harmony, purchasing the enormous cruciform structure used as a hall and assembly room when their community was located there. Part was demolished, but a portion was allowed to stand as an Institute, being 45 feet by 125 feet.

The Harmonites were liberal with their wealth when prosperous. None were turned from their doors hungry. They aided benevolent and educational enterprises. They contributed to the support of families of absent soldiers during the Civil War.

Once when they were in dire distress a merchant extended them credit, and this credit enabled them to get their enterprise on its feet. Many years later conditions were reversed, and this merchant was about to go down before a financial storm. Father Rapp filled two bags with gold coin, rode to the merchant's home, delivered it to him, and told him as much more was ready for him if it was needed.

In its later days the colony became indebted through careless accounting and was on the verge of bankruptcy. Courageously facing facts, accountants were employed, and a financial statement rendered. By the sale of securities and by relentless work, the debts were finally paid. The necessity of careful accounting was made clear, for there was no dishonesty, only a confusion of accounts that hid facts from even those handling the books.

The Harmonites were not a distinct religious sect. They acknowledged no creed except the Bible. They regarded community goods as an essential part of Christianity. They believed in the final restoration of the earth to a condition of paradise. They believed in future rewards and punishments.

The observation seems justified in this colony, as in others that will be studied, that the strong, dominating personality necessary to fix the policies and traditions which are to guide the colony may in time become a weakness; for the colonists lean on such a masterful leader and do not develop the strength and ability which must be present after his death; they look forward to another such leader and are likely to be unwise in the choice, with the result that with everything left to the judgment of this misplaced leader, they may be landed in desperate straits before they know it. There is one perfect example of this in the Swedish Community, founded in 1846, which will be considered in a subsequent chapter.

THE SEPARATISTS OF ZOAR
1819—1898

The followers of Joseph Baumeler, founder of Zoar community, were known as Separatists, for they renounced allegiance to the church and refused to aid the state in military service. They were persecuted in Europe and driven from place to place... One of the leaders was taken before Napoleon, but he told the latter that he "would have to account on judgment day for the multitude of souls he was hurrying to eternity by reason of his bloody wars."

The followers of Baumeler, or Bimeler, as he was later known, came to this country in 1817 and located in Tuscarawas County, Ohio. They worked all winter building houses, and in the spring of 1818 the colony was established at Zoar. Some of the colonists were so poor they could not live in the colony at first, but had to hire out as laborers. Some remained out to learn trades that they might be more useful to the colony when they became resident members.

Common ownership of property was a part of the original program, but the necessity of holding together forced them to it, and they never departed from this rule. This was adopted in 1819, and prosperity attended them from that time on, until they eventually owned thousands of acres of rich land, a sawmill, a woolen factory, a store, a hotel, and other properties worth not less than three quarters of a million dollars in 1870, the peak of their prosperity. They owned sheep, dairy cows, a cattle barn 210 feet long and 50 feet wide with 104 stalls which cost $7,000 and was modern in every respect for the time when it was built.

Each family had a small garden, and in addition there were community gardens, especially a flower garden.

During the Civil War many thousands of dollars were spent to hire substitutes that the young men of the colony might remain at home; but 14 were swept away nevertheless.

The Zoar colony reached its greatest population in 1832 when a large number of emigrants came from Germany, reaching about 500 persons. These were divided into classes. The first class included probationary members, the children, and all who had not signed the covenant. Children reaching majority could be received into the second class after a year's delay by making application. Only members of the second class could vote or hold office, but in other respects they had equal privileges. Many did not care to graduate into the second class, so that a minority actually held the power. But a greater number refused to go into the second class because their private property then became communal property never to be withdrawn. Members of the first class could withdraw whatever property they brought in; but members of the second class who wished to leave would be granted a gift, not as a right, but as a mark of esteem.

Women enjoyed the same right as men in all respects. They pursued such occupations as garden work, field work when strong enough, and knitting.

Besides the working members of the colony, the Zoarites hired outside wage workers. The practice was begun in 1834 when cholera had swept away one third of the population and was not discontinued. It was regarded by some as being bad for the colony, however. The hours of labor were from sunrise to sunset. Groceries and provisions were distributed equally to each family according to the number of persons in the family. Beef was the only meat used. Each family raised poultry, exchanging surplus eggs at the store, or turning them in to be used by those who had an insufficient supply. The rationing of food was not strictly according to needs, considerable latitude being allowed.

The Zoar colony was ruled by three trustees, appointing such subordinates as they considered necessary; but these trustees were responsible to a Standing Committee of Five, to which reports were made and who were consulted on many matters. The Standing Committee was thus the central power, and to it members could appeal from the decisions of the trustees.

The Constitution provided that all officers should be voted for by all of the full members; that one trustee and one member of the Standing Committee should be elected annually; that a cashier should be chosen every four years; and that the time of election should be published 20 days before taking place.

A probation period of one year was required of new members, and during this time they were paid wages. Then if admitted they became members of the first class. The following year they were permitted to join the second class if they felt disposed to do so.

Longevity was also noted among the Zoarites. In 1876 when Mr. Hinds visited the Zoar community, he found a man, who had formerly lived with the Shakers, who was then 93, a woman 93, another woman 87, and a number between 75 and 80. The foreman of one of the factories was past 86, and a member had then recently died at the age of 90.

There was no particular religious belief, tho all of the members were devoutly religious. Contrary to some other colonies, the Zoarites began as celibates, but changed to marriage so that they might have children to carry on the work. It was a rule for a while that children should be taken care of by the Society from the time they were three years old. Many regarded the later departure from this rule as being a step backward.

Social life was almost entirely lacking, though they had some musical organizations. There were no lectures, concerts, or entertainments, and dancing was prohibited as being sinful. There were no higher institutions of learning, and there seemed to be no ideal of encouraging learning. There was no library, and the few books to be found were chiefly on religion.

The religious and social and political principles as set forth by the Zoar-ites, included the following:

"We believe and confess the Trinity of God—Father, Son, and Holy Ghost.

"The return through Christ to God, our proper Father.

"The Holy Scriptures as the measure and guide to our lives and the touchstone of truth and falsehood.

"All ceremonies are banished from among us, and we declare them use-less and injurious, and this is the chief cause of our Separation.

"Our marriages are contracted by mutual consent, and before witnesses. They are notified to the political authority, and we reject all intervention of priests or preachers.

"All intercourse of the sexes, except what is necessary to the per-petuation of the species, we hold to be sinful and contrary to the order and command of God.

"We cannot serve as soldiers because a Christian cannot murder his enemy, much less his friend.

"We regard political government as absolutely necessary to maintain or-der and to protect the good and honest and punish the wrong-doers, and no one can prove us to be untrue to the constituted authorities."

Joseph Ackermann, who served as trustee for more than half a century, and who had chief superintendence of much of the colony when 74 years of age, was not an intellectual man. He admitted to Mr. Hinds that he was discouraged about the future of Zoar. The younger generation had not the same earnestness that controlled the original members. They had fallen into the ways of the world, and would not brook the restraints that religious communism required. And Mr. Hinds comments:

'Evidently it is not enough that a Community have a religious afflatus and intelligent, earnest men at the beginning. It must find means to keep that afflatus alive and strong and to replace its founders, as occasion re-quires, with men of equal intelligence and earnestness * * *

"They had no meetings except on Sunday, and these were not gener-ally attended and were not of a kind to elicit special interest or enthusiasm * * * The women sat on one side and the men on the other * * * A com-munity should be an enlarged home, differing from the small home only in its increased attractions and its greater facilities for improving character. Zoar, at least in its later years, was not a complete community. The prop-erty was held in common; the agricultural and commercial businesses were carried on in common; they had a common church and school house and common customs and principles; but each family had its separate house-hold arrangements; there was no large unitary kitchen nor dining room nor laundry, and in other respects the place resembled more an ordinary coun-try village than a well-organized community. The hotel was thronged after work hours with hirelings and Communists; and as the former drank and smoked and used rough language, it would have been strange indeed if some of the Communists did not fall into like bad habits. **Experience shows that a Community thrives best when some check is placed upon the intercourse of its members with ordinary society."**

The Zoarites had almost as much trouble with seceders as the Harmonists. Their covenant specifically set forth that all property was the property of the community and that none had personal individual rights above that of the community. Two cases in law were won by them which are important. One was a decision by the Supreme Court of the United States, and again showed that no person seceding can force a division of property. The other was in the state court and decided that no member who subscribed to the covenant nor any heir of his should be entitled, in payment for servises, to a divisible share of the property of the Community.

The Zoarites answered the question: What are the advantages you enjoy by reason of your collectivism? by answering:

"The advantages are many and great. All distinctions of rich and poor are abolished. The members have no care except for their own spiritual culture. Collectivism provides for the sick, the weak, the unfortunate, all alike, which makes their life comparatively easy and pleasant. In case of great loss by fire or flood or other cause, the burden which would be ruinous to one is easily borne by the many. Charity and genuine love one to another, which are the foundations of true Christianity, can be more readily cultivated and practiced in collectivism than in common, isolated society. Finally, a community is the best place in which to get rid of selfishness, willfulness, and bad habits and vices generally; for we are subject to the constant surveillance and reproof of others, which, rightly taken, will go far toward preparing us for the large Community above."

But the young people did not have the same faith as the elders, and this eventually led to a division of the property and a return to individual ownership. Three disinterested persons made the division, which proved to be entirely satisfactory to all. The dominating force which had urged them forward under Bimeler and Ackermann were lacking, and the business had ceased to prosper.

In the division—there were 222 persons in the colony at the time—only full members could share; but as there were eleven first-class members eligible to second class, these were advanced in the interests of peace. This made the total 233 who participated, the remainder being children. However, some young people were made certain allowances also. At the time of the division the colony possessed 7300 acres of land assessed at $340,820, and other property worth $16,250. The sale of timber lands resulted in $15,000 to the colony and provided for the expenses of the division, besides allotting $200 to each full member. The full amount was about $2500 when the entire division was made.

"Zoar was the most democratic of the so-called religious communities," says Mr. Hinds in his 'American Communities.' "Its constitution was subject to amendment by a two-thirds vote. Its elections were conducted in accordance with the laws of the state. All officials were elective. Elective members could be recalled at any time. There was no religious hierarchy and any form of aristocracy was carefully guarded against.

One of its Articles of Agreement stated that:

"As peace and unity can be maintained only by a general equality among the members, it is therefore severally understood and declared that no extra demands shall be made or allowed in respect to meat, drink, clothing, dwellings, etc.,', and the preamble adopted in 1833 affirmed:"All inequalities and distinctions of rank and fortune shall be abolished from amongst us, that we may live as brethren and and sisters of one common family."

ROBERT OWEN AND HIS COMMUNITIES
(1825 — 1827)

Perhaps the Community given most general publicity, though about which there is a great deal of misapprehension, is the New Harmony colony, the greatest of the Owen experiments.

Robert Owen, known as the "Father of Socialism," had world-wide schemes which attracted almost universal attention in the early part of the nineteenth century. He was the first to advocate the shortening of hours of work in English factories; his was the first factory to establish the ten-hour day—then a far more radical thing than the six-hour-day, five-day-week proposal of to-day. He thought eight hours would be enough eventually. He first instituted legislation in behalf of women and children which made it impossible to employ children of six, as had been done. He founded the first infant schools and established the kindergarten. He built model lodging houses, public baths, "ragged" schools, "elder" schools, and other projects to help the working people. He was almost a century ahead of others in seeing the necessity of such work. Though he may be looked upon now as a reformer, he stood then as a su per-radical in his demands.

At one time he gave one third ot his fortune to the aid of an educational scheme. He subscribed $50,000 in an effort to help the working classes. When his Equitable Bank failed, he shouldered the entire debt, tho he was not responsible for it. The bank had not been a profit-making device, but one for the assistance of workers, which, it was hoped, would prevent unemployment.

When the New Harmony colony failed, he paid all of its debts and left $3,000 as a contribution to the education of its children. He paid his operatives in his cotton mills full wages for four years when the mills shut down during the American embargo on cotton. It was his suggestion that five per cent of the profits be deducted and the rest be used in educational work.

Owen became manager of the New Lanark cotton mills when only 28 years old. He at once abolished pauper labor—it had been the system to ship in pauper children as mill hands, sometimes as many as 500 being thus employed. He induced people to quit pilfering; drunkenness became an exception in the village of New Lanark; the quality of food and clothing used by operatives was greatly improved, and the cost reduced 25 per cent; hours of labor were reduced and wages increased; schools for different ages were instituted; amusements, military exercises and dancing were introduced; lecture courses were arranged. His village became far ahead of others in morals, cleanliness, healthfulness, happiness, and prosperity.

His fame spread so far that dukes and kings consulted him and Tsar Nicholas of Russia stopped for two days as a visitor in Owen's house, trying to induce Owen to go to Russia.

It was Owen's opinion that "human nature is radically good and is capable of being trained, educated, and placed from birth in such a manner that all ultimately become united, good, wise, healthy, and happy." This opinion was generally accepted; but, when Owen launched an attack on religion, he drew the dislike, then the hatred, of the entire religious world, which had no little power at that time.

In 1820 Owen published a work on the results of his work at New Lanark with a scheme for a rational reconstruction of society. He proposed to cut the world up into villages of 300 to 2000 persons, preferring about 800 to 1200. His plan was semi-collectivism, but he allowed a small acreage to each family

It was in 1825 that Robert Owen came to the United States and purchased the Harmony community from the Rappites, securing the 30,000 acres of land and the result of ten years work with buildings and orchards and vineyards and roads and a greater value than was represented in the purchase price of $100,000. He invited the people of all nations to participate, explaining that it was no move on his part to increase his own wealth. He even delivered lectures in the House of Representatives in the presence of the president, president-elect, members of Congress, and many others.

Within a space of six weeks a population of 800 persons was drawn together, and in October, 1925, the number was 900. Other societies, taking inspiration from New Harmony, were established in nine other places. Most of them were very short-lived. The capital of the New Harmony colony was $150,000, and everything was in readiness to go ahead, so far as material matters were concerned. Many prominent educators and scientists, later to make their fame secure, were associated in this work. The Owen family became residents of this country, and attained national fame, three of them in the second, and one in the third generation.

In 1826 the community was given a new constitution which was expected to adjust all difficulties which might arise; but it seems to have had quite the contrary effect. The government was in the hands of a Committee of Six. A General Assembly soon asked the Executive Council to request the aid of Owen for one year in conducting the affairs of the community. But Owen could not remain, and the colony fell into bad ways. Several splits followed, and attempts to form new colonies. Dissatisfaction became greater and greater. The end soon came.

Many reasons are given for the failure. One ascribes it to the absence of Owen during the early days of the community, when his presence was most needed. Another describes the dishonesty of one Taylor. Another attributes it to anxiety regarding individual property. Still another thought "it is impossible to carry out a communistic system unless in a place utterly removed from contact with the world, or with the help of some powerful re-

ligious conviction. Mere benevolence, mere sentiments of universal phil-
anthropy are far too weak to bind the self-seeking affections of men."

Robert Dale Owen, son of Robert Owen, said his father made a mistake in
not establishing his community in England and a greater mistake in admitting
all comers into membership, without recommendation or examination whatever. He once said: "At New Harmony there was not disinterested industry,
there was not mutual confidence, there was not practical experience, there
was no union of action, because there was not unanimity of counsel; and
these were the points of difference and dissension — the rocks on which the
social bark struck and was wrecked."

Robert Owen himself said that he "wanted honesty of purpose and got
dishonesty; wanted temperance and got intemperance; wanted industry and
found idleness; wanted cleanliness and found dirt; wanted carefulness and
found waste; wanted fine desire for knowledge and found apathy * * *"

**"In justice to the memory of Robert Owen it should be stated," says Hinds,
"that late in life he ceased to be a mere materialist, and confessed that he
then saw (what he had in previous life overlooked) the necessity of good
spiritual conditions in forming the character of man, and that 'these are the
most important of all in the future development of mankind.'"**

Horace Greeley and Chas. A. Dana attributed the failure of New Harmony to the lack of a religious basis upon which all successful communities
have been founded — Owen having been the first to attempt the establishment of a non-religious community. Greeley said that a great obstacle en-
countered in such experiments was "the class of people attracted—the con-
ceited, the crochety, and the selfish"; while Dana concluded: "Destroy self-
hood and you destroy all motive to exertion."

Others who were associated with Owen give various reasons, according
to Lockwood. One said: "He found democrats harder to manage than the
servile workmen of Scotland." Another reported that "the Owenites were
too independent"; while a third thought that he "did not have enough depu-
ties." C. W. Burt believed that "Communism must be ruled either by law or
grace."

In summing up the reasons for the failure of the Owen colony, there
are several conditions which should be considered. Eight hundred or nine
hundred persons thrown together to carry out an untried scheme, most of
them inexperienced in things practical, many of them carried by fine sentiments instead of deep convictions, perhaps a majority intent on bettering
their personal condition rather than pursuing a principle, and all of them
strangers to one another and likely to be hostile and suspicious— these alone
are enough to make a problem. When, then, Owen was absent, so that the
initial energy was lacking and he had to depend on those less conversant
with his plan and less skilful and able, it is not surprising that trouble quickly ensued.

Accepting as members all who came, without examination or investigation, and without requiring them to pay anything, is almost certain of gathering together people of weak purpose and little principle, those most likely to be ready to throttle the entire enterprise for their own personal gain.

Besides this, there was no general understanding, though there may have been a superficial knowledge, of the plan and the principles of the Owen enterprise. There was no continued plan of careful preliminary education in colony methods.

But perhaps most important of all was the lack of a conviction strong enough to carry it through the period of organization, the period when the new had worn off, and when the spectacular features had begun to abate. Collectivism, as may be observed by the examples given of various colonies, must have the strength of a religious conviction, and be carried through with a religious fervor. It need not have any religious significance, and may have not even a place of worship; but it must be the religion itself in the absence of any other. The cohesive power of collectivism insures success when those who espouse it do so from principle; but when this espousal is from mere hope for personal rewards, aggrandizement, ease, or security, the members are likely to destroy the institution they hope to build by reason of the selfishness of their personal desires and motives, and their actions growing out of those motives and selfish desires.

Yet, although the colony as a whole was not a success, it established certain standards and was noteworthy in many ways.

Among the outgrowths of the unfortunate New Harmony colony of Robert Owen, was the Nashoba Colony, near Memphis, which was launched by Frances Wright, who was associated with Robert Owen and Robert Dale Owen and later with William Owen. Francis Wright intended this to elevate the negroes, but it was founded on slavery and never developed as its founders expected. Later Francis Wright was associated with the New Harmony movement, and a quarter of a century later founded what eventually became the first genuine woman's club. She toured the country lecturing on equality for the sexes, and making particularly strong attacks on the unjust property laws which put men legally much above women. She was the first to talk for equal suffrage and attracted widespread attention.

New Harmony took the lead in prohibition of the liquor traffic, in equality of men and women, liberalism in religious views, and education.

Mr. Owen said: "The greatest waste and loss result from the disunited minds and feelings of mankind. Armies, churches, lawyers, doctors, and exclusive universities are the greatest obstacles to progress * * * There is great loss from the separation of the trades and the expense of exchange and transportation * * *"

"The practice of the rational religion will consist in promoting, to the utmost of our power, the happiness and well-being of every man, woman, and child, without regard to their sect, party, or color; and its worship, in these inexpressible feelings of wonder, admiration, and delight, which, when man is surrounded by superior circumstances only, will naturally arise from the contemplation of the infinity of space, of the eternity of duration, of the order of the universe, and of that Incomprehensible Power by which the atom is moved and the aggregate of nature is governed."

There is no questioning the fact that New Harmony was far ahead of its time in many of its institutions. It established the first infant school in America in 1826; the first kindergarten of any type in the Western World; the first use of the kindergarten as a part of the public school system; the first distinctly trade school, and the second industrial school; the first industrial school of any type to be made a part of the free public school system; the first free public school system; the first real public school west of the Appalachian mountains.

It seems as a fitting climax to the Owen activities — for the Owen family became well known, even famous in the second generation — that Rich-Owen died at the age of 81 at New Harmony in 1890.

"Whatever may be thought of Robert Owen's theories, schemes, and experiments," comments Hinds, "his motives were of the noblest. Not personal aggrandizement, but the good of humanity, was the central, dominant object of his life. In his own words: 'Crown, coronet, mitres, military displays, pomp of war, wide colonies, and a huge empire are, in my view, all trifles light as air unless with them you can have a fair share of contentment, comfort, and happiness among the great body of the people.' "

HOPEDALE COMMUNITY
(1842—1868)

The Hopedale Community, originally called Fraternal Community No 1, was formed at Mendon, Massachusetts, January 28, 1841, by about thirty individuals from different parts of the state, and began operations in 1842. It attained a total population of 275 persons, had 800 acres of land, thirty dwelling houses, three mechanic shops, water power, woodworking and other machinery, and a small chapel also used as a school house, and barns and outbuildings.

It was a Fourier experiment and was organized by Rev. Adin Ballou, who put his entire energy into it. The failure of the colony in 1868 almost proved the death of the founder, who was a man of the finest sentiments, and one who worked mentally and physically to make the colony a success.

The colony was founded on religious principles, and a description of it written at the time says: It is an educational society, preparing to act an important part in the training of the young. It is a socialistic Community, successfully actualizing as well as promulgating practical Christian Socialism — the only kind of socialism likely to establish a true social state on earth. It guarantees to all of its members and dependents employment, at least adequate to a comfortable subsistence, relief in want, sickness, and distress, decent opportunities for religious, moral, and intellectual culture, an orderly and well-regulated neighborhood * * *"

It was originally expected that Hopedale should be but one of a chain of colonies in all parts of the world, "co-ordinated and organically united in a great federation styled "The Practical Christian Communism." This was changed to give complete attention to Hopedale alone, for this would demand the entire attention of all able persons in it.

The government of the Hopedale Community was placed in the hands of three trustees, who were to account directly to the whole body of their fellow associates. But many long-drawn-out discussions were still held and there was much criticism, so that monthly meetings were held for Christian discipline and improvement. Action was taken at them on instances of conduct of members when this did not meet with general approval. It must have been similar to the General Assembly of other colonies, and akin to the Mutual Criticism of the Oneida Community.

Industrial and financial improvement followed, and in 1852 the treasurer's report was so glowing that a general celebration was held. Adin Ballou thought it time to retire as president, after his years of organizing and managing and hard physical work along with the rest of them. But almost immediately misfortunes began to set in. A benefactor of the community, Susan Fish, died, and the son of Adin Ballou also passed away in his 19th year. Two of the oldest members of the community died soon after. A free love episode gave great notoriety to the colony and disturbed the members, though the offenders were forced to leave.

But in spite of these misfortunes, the community thrived, and plans were made for a branch colony in Minnesota. This effort was a failure, however. In 1856 the colony showed a deficit of $145, besides passing dividends on stock, amounting to $1652. Depreciation had not been allowed for, either, so that the deficit was really serious, and finally a firm which had secured three fourths of the stock took charge of it.

"The Hopedale Community," says Hinds, "was an attempt to combine individual and common interests, the members being permitted to hold property and carry on business independently of the Community; and it is noteworthy fact that at least in the case of (the firm which forclosed the colony), their individual interests, even when one of them was President and the other Treasurer, yielded them larger profits than the entire profits of the Community, being in 1855 over $7000, and such individual business must have absorbed a large share of their attention, and correspondingly diverted it from the Community's business; and a record is yet to be found of a Community that attained permanent success under such a handicap of rampant individualism." This was also Ballou's summary.

The wonder is that the community existed so long under such conditions. It tried to pay interest on the investment, which was far from being the spirit of collectivist communities, and it permitted a very unequal ownership of interests in the community. With the machinery of capitalistic or competitive business a part of the colony, and special inducements held out to make use of it to the benfits of individuals rather than to the community, it is no wonder that the community did not prosper, but it is marvelous that it was able to go so long under such conditions.

FOURIER AND HIS EXPERIMENTS

Charles Fourier of France and his scheme of social regeneration inflamed the imagination of hundreds of thousands of people on both sides of the Atlantic. In 1842 he arranged for the full control of a column in the daily New York Tribune, and for more than a year filled it with matter of interest to thousands of readers. His plan commanded a large share of public attention and Albert Brisbane and Horace Greeley were in hearty accord with it. Six colonies or associations or "phalanxes," as they were called, were formed in Ohio, seven in New York, six in Pennsylvania, two in Massachusetts, two in Illinois, two in New Jersey, one in Michigan, three in Wisconsin, and one in Indiana — a total of 30 in all.

Ten of them failed to finish the first year, seven failed to finish the second year, three did not reach the third year, and all the rest had failed before the sixth year, with the exception of the North American Phalanx above noted. The list as given by Mr. Hinds in "American Communities," shows thirty communities formed during this period.

	State	Memb.	Acres	Begun	Duration Years
Alphadelphia Phalanx	Mich.	200	2814	1844	2¾
Bloomfield Association	N. Y.	148	500	1844	1½
Brook Farm Community	Mass.	115	200	1841	½
Bureau County Phalanx	Ill.	?	?	1843	?
Clarkson Industrial Association	N. Y.	420	2000	1844	½
Clermont Phalanx	Ohio	120	900	1844	2½
Columbia Phalanx	Ohio	128	large	1844	1
Goose Pond Community	Penn.	60	2000	1844	—
Integral Phalanx	Ill.	120	508	1845	1½
Jefferson Co. Indu. Assn.	N. Y.	400	1200	1843	1
La Grange Phalanx	Ind.	120	1045	1844	2
Leraysville Phalanx	Penn.	40	1500	1844	¾
McKean Co. Assn.	Penn.	?	30,000	1843	?
Marlboro Association	Ohio	24	?	1841	4
Moorehouse Union	N. Y.	?	?	1843	1
North American Phalanx	N. J.	112	673	1843	13
Northampton Association	Mass.	130	500	1842	4
Ohio Phalanx	Ohio	100	2200	1844	¾
One-Mention Community	Penn.	40	800	1843	1
Ontario Community	N. Y.	150	150	1844	?
Prairie Home Community	Ohio	130	500	1843	1
Raritan Bay Union	N. J.	—	268	1853	?
Social Reform Unity	Penn.	20	2000	1842	¾
Sodus Bay Phalanx	N. Y.	300	1400	1844	—mo
Spring Farm Association	Wis.	40	—	1846	3
Sylvania Association	Penn.	145	2393	1843	2
Trumbull Phalanx	Ohio	200	1500	1844	3
Unitarian Association	Wis.	200	—	1844	½
Western N. Y. Indust. Assn.	N. Y.	350	1400	1844	—
Wisconsin Phalanx	Wis.	180	1800	1844	6

(Information from Hinds' "American Communities")

There were apparently others not on this list. As Hinds comments, "The projectors had more zeal than wisdom, and the hope of better social conditions is so strong in the human heart that people are easily induced to risk everything in their attempted realization."

Four of these projects, however, are worthy of some attention. These are Brook Farm, perhaps one of the best know in history; the North American Phalanx; Northampton Association; and the Wisconsin Phalanx. Though Fourier furnished the inspiration for these communities, he was not responsible for their being started, and they did not become demonstrations of his ideas.

Brook Farm — 1841 - 1847

Brook Farm was organized in 1841 and gathered together orators, philosophers, poets, authors. It numbered some of the most famous men in American letters as its members. Perhaps best known of them is Nathaniel Hawthorne, who wrote concerning Brook Farm:

" * * * We meant to lessen the laboring man's great burden of toil by performing our due share of it at the cost of our own thews and sinews. We sought our profit by mutual aid, instead of wresting it by the strong hand of the enemy, or filching it craftily from those less shrewd than ourselves (if indeed there are any such in New England), or winning it by selfish competition with a neighbor; in one or another of which fashions every son of woman both perpetrates and suffers his share of the common evil, whether he chooses it or not. * * * "

Brook Farm does not owe its origin to Fourierism, but to Transcendentalism and was the outgrowth of an organization of cultured Boston people. Rev. George Ripley was the founder; he was a minister in a Unitarian church.

The plan of organization was the common ownership of industries, equal wages, a common guaranty of support of all members, their children and family dependents, house rent, food, clothing, and other necessaries furnished without cost exceeding a certain amount fixed annually by the members. No charge was made for support during inability to labor from sickness or old-age, except to share-holders, and then not to exceed interest on their shares. No charge was made for education. Shares of stock were $100 with interest at 5 per cent guaranteed.

In 1844 the community became a Fourier organization. The community was incorporated. And the government of it consisted of a General Council consisting of the Council of Industry of five members; a council of Finance with four members; a Council of Science with three members; and the Central Council formed of the President and the chairman of the other three councils. There were Series of Workers, as the Farming Series, the Mechanical Series, the Domestic Series, each Series being composed of groups. Thus the Farming Series had a Cattle Group, a Milking Group, a Plowing Group, a Nursery Group, a Planting Group, a Hoeing Group, a Weeding Group, a Haying Group, etc. In a community of 70 members this cumbersome machinery of government. must have greatly interfered with efficiency.

Brook Farm was not a financial success. There was a dearth of workers. However, there were numerous applications for membership, though many of the applicants were totally unfitted for such an enterprise. Four thousand visitors came in one year. Industries did not pay. The burning of a building under construction after $7000 had been spent on it was depressing, and one by one the members lost heart and left.

THE NORTH AMERICAN PHALANX — (1843 to 1856)

This was organized on August 12, 1843, and began practical operations in September of the same year. It was the longest-lived of all the Fourier experiments, surviving until January, 1856.

In a letter published in December, 1844, it was said that the colony had finished a dwelling to accommodate 100 persons, each family having a parlor and two bedrooms, and that there was in operation a blacksmith shop and machine shop and a saw mill. Four hundred acres of land were ready for cultivation.

In 1854 the New York Tribune published an article in which it was stated: "The domain consists of 673 acres, and there is a flour mill and saw mill, a mansion house, a two-story brick building, besides carpenter shops and a blacksmith shop. * * * The domain with all of its improvements is valued at $67,350. The phalanx numbers about 100 members. Labor is credited by the hour. Each person is charged with his board, lodging, and whatever he receives from the association, and the balance due is paid. All eat in the same dining hall; a bill of fare is made out as at an eating house, and every one orders what he likes and is charged accordingly. * * * The business of drying fruit is carried on to some extent. Some kinds of fruit are bottled. * * * They have 70 acres of apple and peach trees and raise large crops of potatoes, tomatoes, turnips, melons, cucumbers, and garden seeds. Wheat, rye, and buckwheat flour, cornmeal, samp, and hominy are manufactured and sold in New York."

The end of the colony was unexpected, and seems not to be fully explained by the information available. The members had gathered to erect a new mill, and while they were trying to decide on a location, some one raised the question as to whether there was any use in going further with the experiment. A vote was taken, and a majority was found to be in favor of dissolution. The property was sold at forced sale, bringing only 65 cents on the dollar, despite the fact that the stock had paid a fair dividend for several years; the rate being between four and five per cent, in addition to wages to members and workers.

The colony had existed for more than 12 years and had passed thru the preliminary trials. They spent the days in labor and the nights in legislation for the first five years, but had passed thru that period. They were financially successful. Hinds asks:

"What did break it up? No one has given a satisfactory answer. The burning of the mill, which was the immediate occasion, was no sufficient cause of the break up, as Horace Greeley offered to loan $12,000 to build a new one. There was some religious controversy * * * there was some evil thinking of the stock-holders; there was a lack of educational facilities. Bucklin, one of its presidents, considered that its wage-regulation was the principal cause of the dissolution, too little difference being made between the labor of brain and muscle. He said the chief of the agricultural department received only ten cents an hour; a skilful teacher received only nine cents, but was able to go outside and receive $5 for only two hours' work. A foreman received only five or ten cents more than other workers.

"But all this talk," comments Hinds, "about wage troubles, to my mind, only proves that the great objects which originally drew the members together had lost their first power over them and that lower and more material considerations were becoming dominant in their minds and hearts. That is usually, perhaps always, the case when any such organization starts on its downward course; and, alas! there are too few eager to call the attention of the faint-hearted to the fact that the Society was organized for the very purpose of destroying such wage and wealth distinctions as they now cover, and could not exist without them; and that the sweetest joy in this world comes, not from riches and what riches can procure, but from sharing life's burdens with others * * *. When this sentiment was wholly displaced in a Phalanx, Association, or Community, it is about time to make arrangements with the undertakers."

It is quite apparent, however, that a community organized to carry into effect the principles of collectivism, but which pays interest on money invested or dividends on stock, and besides this makes differences in wages, had set up divisions which do not give it much advantage over the world of competition, and which bring certain disadvantages. It shows a remarkable tenacity of life that it existed for so many years under conditions that seem to have held with the Colony the seeds of dissolution.

The Northampton Association — 1842 - 1846

Samuel L. Hill was among the founders of this colony, for a time treasurer, and a continuous member. Its full name was The Northampton Association of Education and Industry. It was organized in 1842 at Northampton, Mass., and existed for five years. It had 500 acres of land, and for a time one of the industries was growing silk, as there were many mulberry trees on the estate. The total cash investment was $20,000. The colony school was successful, existing during the entire life of the colony, with some pupils sent from other places. Among the colonists were educated men and women and some professional people; a majority were middle-class, substantial people. All worked with hands as well as brains, and they never had any serious trouble in getting the most menial tasks performed, though there may have been some jealousy between the less educated and the more intellectual as there is likely to be in any form of society, collective or otherwise. The Colony had from 130 to 140 members. The management was democratic, both men and women being invited to propose and discuss measures. Wages were paid from the beginning. All ate at a common table. Food and lights were charged at about 50 cents a week at the boarding house and from 75 cents to $1.00 a week in private houses. Religion had no part in colony life; some were religious, some were not. There was some friction when ministers were brought in to meetings, as the agreement also permitted free discussion and resulted in dissatisfaction. Some members withdrew, taking capital with them.

Lack of sufficient capital was given as the cause of the final disbandment of the colony. The management of the division of the estate was so careful that no money was lost. The members lost their time, and whatever chances they might otherwise have had for personal advancement, but most of them considered the experience worth it, probably, as many so expressed themselves.

THE WISCONSIN PHALANX — (1844—1850)

On Saturday, May 25, 1844, nineteen men and one boy entered the Ceresco Valley in Fond-du-Lac County, Wisconsin to establish the Wisconsin Phalanx. The nearest sawmill was 22 miles away, and they built their first houses of split logs. Sixteen families went through the first winter with only two buildings 20 x 30 feet and one and one-half stories high. In 1846 there were 180 resident members, mostly of the working class, with no lawyers, doctors, or ministers among them, though there were men of much ability in the group.

At the end of each year an appraisal of property was made, and one fourth of the ascertained profits went to capital and the remaining three fourths to the members, according to the number of hours of labor put in. Board was charged at cost, and never exceeded 75 cents a week. The colony was financially successful, paying eight per cent to stockholders in 1850. Ten thousand bushels of wheat were raised one season. No intoxicating drinks were allowed to be sold, and there was never a lawsuit. Religious sects were tolerated.

Hinds quotes Everett Chamberlain as follows: "There was a faithful attempt to carry out the complicated plan of Fourier in personal credits and the equalization of labor by reducing all to what was called the class of usefulness; and under this arrangement some of the most skilled workmen were able to score as many as 25 hours labor in one day — a paradox in time-keeping which was exceedingly amusing to the skillful ones and correspondingly perplexing to the unskillful, since everybody drew stock or cash on settlement day in proportion to his credit on the daily record."

Warren Chase, leader in the enterprise is quoted as follows: "It was a social failure largely because we could not at the time make the home attractive and pleasant. Many thought they could do better with their means on the outside. We could not induce others with means to join us and purchase the stock of the discontented * * * A little town which had grown up near us with whiskey shops became a great annoyance and with its prejudice, falsehoods, and abuse greatly aided in the dissolution of the Phalanx * * *" He also says that the property qualification was a bad thing as they "often rejected the better and accepted the worse because the worse had the property qualification." Another explained the cause of failure as being speculation—"the love of money and the want of love for association."

"It would be interesting to group together all the reasons which have been given for the non-success of associate experiments," says Hinds; "and it would be no less interesting to note that many of them possessed the very conditions deemed the most essential to success by others. How many of the Phalanxes and communities which have come to premature death have ascribed their mortality to a debt or poor land or sickness or laziness or quarrels about property titles or leadership, or religion, or to sexual irregularities? But the Wisconsin Phalanx was always free from debt, had a splendid domain of 1800 acres, was in a healthful climate, had no trouble with lazy ones worth mentioning, had no quarrel about land titles, its principal founder maintaining throughout the experiment the confidence of the members; religious differences created no trouble—and still it failed like the rest."

Noyes, in his "History of American Socialism," after reviewing the experience of the Phalanx concluded that "the coroner's verdict must be: Died —not by any of the common diseases of Associations; such as poverty, dissension, lack of wisdom, mortality, or religion, but by deliberate suicide for reasons not fully disclosed."

However, those who have had experience and have keenly observed co-operatives and Communities will not hesitate to put their finger on at least one cause — the one pointed out by the writer who said that the "love of money and want of love for the association * * *" In a form of society where unequal allotments are made, no matter what the excuse or reason or how fine the system, dissatisfaction is certain to follow, and these unequal rewards result in a superior class with opportunities for greater leisure, and an inferior class ~~class~~ which will feel it is being oppressed. The surprising thing is that such a society should have lived so long. A Community depends on the spirit of its members, and when conditions are such that they pin their faith and hopes and shape their ends toward individual advantages and benefits, the essential spirit of co-operation and the cohesiveness necessary to success must be lacking, and failure is a matter of time only.

A COMMUNITY OF SWEDES
1846—1862

Eric Janson, a native of Sweden, received a vision which instructed him to do certain things and which also miraculously cured him of a severe attack of rheumatism. He became a religious leader and attracted a considerable following, which was subjected to much persecution. Janson was charged with atrocious crimes and stood trial, but defended himself successfully. His fame grew, and the people deserted the churches to follow Janson. The incensed clergy had Janson arrested six times. The king, before whom Janson was brought twice, had him freed each time, but the clergy continued their persecution, until Janson left Sweden for America to found a Community. A disciple, Olaf Olson, had come in advance to find a suitable location.

The first colonists arrived in 1846 and part of them made much of the journey to Henry County, Illinois, by foot, where they established the Bishop Hill Community. They acquired an improved farm of 80 acres, but the rest of the land was unbroken virgin soil. The colonists dug caves in narrow ravines and roofed them over with poles covered with sod, living in them for several years. Their fare was scanty and coarse. They were harrassed by fevers, and finally cholera took 114 inside of two weeks.

One of the first buildings erected was a log church large enough to accommodate 1000 persons. Twelve young men were given a short course in English and sent out to carry on evangelical work. In the Community work was carried on during most of the daylight hours. There were no amusements, no beauty. Without money or credit they went forward despite disease and hardships, though 200 left in 1848, because they could not agree with Janson's claims as a religious prophet.

However, harvests were bountiful, and buildings of adobe, sun-dried and burned brick, were put up. One of the brick structures was four stories in height, 100 feet long, and 45 feet wide. They bought timber lands and put up a sawmill. Health improved with better food and better living conditions.

One John Root, an educated Swede, and Mexican war veteran, was allowed to marry a cousin in the Colony. Against the written stipulation that he should never take her from the colony, he attempted to do so.

When she refused, he resorted to force on two occasions. Both times she was rescued and brought back. At one time, by relays of horses, the 150-mile rescue trip was made without a stop. Root returned, gathered a mob, and proposed storming the Community; but neighbors gathered in defense of the colonists, whom they esteemed for their industriousness. Root pushed legal proceedings against Janson, and during a noon recess entered the court room and shot Janson. The effect on the Community was extremely bad; for they had looked on their leader as one who would not die. For a time many expected that Janson would return to life.

The colony at this time numbered one thousand people. The leadership passed to others, but the Community continued to prosper. Hinds says: "It owned thousands of acres of fertile land, had a hundred horses, sixty yoke of oxen, large droves of cattle, abundance of food. They cultivated immense fields, having one year 700 acres of broom corn. They erected large brick dwellings, a church and hotel, a large flour mill, work shops, school houses * * * Their 100-foot, four-story brick building was extended to 200 feet. The first floor was used as a common kitchen, the second as a common dining room, and the whole community ate in this room. The upper stories were used as dormitories. Other buildings were put up, including some used at various points during the farming season to save time and labor.

A Board of seven trustees was to hold office during good behavior, subject to a majority vote of the male members of the Community. A full report was made to the members once each year, in January, at which general business was discussed. The colony was prosperous in every way. Hinds comments:

"This experiment certainly possessed many of the elements of permanent success. It had good material in the religious character of its members. It had the qualities which Owen vainly sought, such as economy, industry, honesty, and good morals. Why, then, did it come to such an untimely end? I asked this question many times * * * The death of Eric Janson doubtless shortened its career. * * * He had unlimited control over the temporal as well as spiritual interests of the colony, and allowed no one to question his wisdom. 'It is according to the will of God' silenced all controversy. He believed that he alone had the whole truth and that all people who had not received his views were in darkness.

"Such fanaticism admits of no justification. If it be offered in extenuation that other Community founders have been equally fanatical and that their position of absolute, unquestioned authority in matters temporal and spiritual naturally engenders spiritual pride and fanaticism in them, and flattery and idolatry in their followers, it only follows that thus far the position is a false one, and detrimental to the best interests of all classes affected by it"

The seven trustees were nominally in control of affairs, but an interloper, one Olaf Janson (not related to Eric Janson the founder) got control. While farming and industrial work was bringing increased riches, this new Janson led into foreign speculation, investing in stock in other enterprises, in a coal mine, real estate, bank stock. In one venture alone $34,000 was lost, while in many others the losses were considerable. These things produced discontent, but the members had been taught to have such unquestioned faith in their leaders they they did not rebel, even when they chafed, at the things which were being done. To boldly question this Janson's proceedings would be to incur the dislike of the community, which would have regarded it as sinful.

Finally resolutions were passed by the Community at its annual meeting requiring more conservative management; but the unscrupulous Janson, after being deposed from office in 1860, managed to retain enough influence so that he was appointed with friends to act as receiver in closing up the affairs of the colony in 1862. In this division each adult male and female received 20 acres of land or equivalent value, and the children some property. Religious dissension had set in, however, previous to this, and the colonists, in their rigorous lives and narrow beliefs, had failed to enlist the children's interest, with the result that many of them were leaving the colony.

Here is an example of a colony which was materially successful, which triumphed over great odds, and which seemed to have the foundation to endure. Yet the pendulum swung as far to the right in this case as it did to the left in other colonies of a secular nature — the suspicion which was so rife in some colonies that it wrecked them, was in the instance of the Swedes replaced by a blind faith that left them defenseless when a little ordinary business caution might have saved them. They viewed with abhorrence any questioning of the leaders, with the result that the unscrupulous Olaf Janson ruined the enterprise established by the devout and devoted Eric Janson.

Instead of developing leadership, the first Janson had permitted a blind faith in his ability to grow, so that the colonists were little more than children in executive, legislative, and business affairs. His dominating personality, so essential at first, became in time the very thing which was probably the principal factor in causing the colony to fail.

The Community which fails to develop a sturdy independence of thought —which need not by any means breed disharmony—must depend on strong leaders; and its chances for securing strong leaders devoted to the ideals of the Community are remarkably small if such leaders cannot be developed within the Community.

A SUCCESSFUL SMALL COLONY
1856—1879

That there have been co-operative Communities which have not at-attracted wide attention, but which have nevertheless been entirely successful, is unquestioned. A letter from Mr. James Madison gives a brief synopsis of one. It is perhaps not important as a colony, but it is important as an example of how success was achieved, and of how it left its lasting impress on the people. This last virtue justifies giving space to it.

Mr. Madison went to teach school in a little hamlet, Germania, in Wisconsin. "The little town was unusually friendly and co-operative," he writes. "I inquired into the history of the town and the residents seemed proud to tell me about it. I lived at the residence of State Senator C. E. Pierce. He died last year and was the last member of the Germania Company. This company was a co-operative colony. In 1857 a group of people consisting of about 15 families, headed by Benjamin Hall, left Groton, Massachusetts and established themselves at Germania, Marquette County, Wisconsin. They were followers of Reverend Miller and therefore Second Adventists. The land in the vicinity was purchased from settlers and a large Community House was erected, with apartments to accommodate the several families. The dining room, kitchen, and meeting rooms were common for all. Prayer meetings were held every evening.

"All industries were run in common, each one doing what he could for the common weal. The industries, aside from the large farm of about 1200 acres, were a flour mill, cooper shop, wagon and blacksmith shop, harness and shoe making, and general store.

"Mr. Hall died in 1879, and at the time of the death of Mrs. Hall, the mother of Senator Pierce, the colony divided up the property and the Community ceased as a Colony. However, the advantages of Comunity life, co-operating in most things, left its impress upon the former members and upon the neighbors as well.

"The reason for the Colony discontinuing was that the founders had all passed away and the younger members had raised families of their own. The religious life ceased to hold them, so they were attracted in different directions as their interests directed."

This brief description of a small colony again shows the necessity of a wider urge than the merely religious one of a colony sufficient unto itself. The failure to hold the young folks—recorded in the history of many colonies as a contributing factor toward its being discontinued, even though highly successful in a material way—is of course one which finds its parallel to-day in the young people leaving the farms and the small towns for the cities. But it strikingly shows the necessity of making the community something more than a self-centered group. Perhaps the remedy may be found in a number of colonies with free interchange of colonists, so that the lure of adventure may be satisfied without losing the young people. Or there may be another solution in quite another direction, found through inculcating certain principles. This seems only a part of it, however, for some colonies in the past have made careful and well-organized efforts along this line with only indifferent success. It is clear that here lies a problem which has not been given the attention it must have, and the solution of it will greatly lengthen the lives of Communities.

THE ICARIANS
1848—1895

While many successful Communities were established by religious enthusiasts, it remained for the Icarians, far from being religious, to establish settlements in which collective living was well developed and which survived for more than a quarter of a century. They seemed almost to prove that a desire for mere material welfare and the idealism that has nothing to do with religion would hold to success as well as other and more religious ideals. Yet the Icarians can be said to have proven quite conclusively, on careful analysis, that a devotion to collectivism as an end is not enough, but that it must become an ideal viewed with almost religious fervor if it is to succeed against the selfishness that is certain to crop out of collectivism for purely personal benefits.

Etienne Cabet was the Icarian leader. He had thousands of followers on both sides of the Atlantic. He was a radical who held many offices under the government, though some of them for short times only because of his uncompromising radicalism. He was exiled from France for five years and went to Belgium, where he was again exiled, going to England. Returning to France, he devoted himself to the cause of Communism. His teachings spread over France and roused the opposition of the government, the priesthood, the police, the courts, and the press. In 1847 there were hundreds of thousands of followers of Cabet in France, Switzerland, Spain, Germany, England, and other countries. When in 1847 he announced that Communism was to be tried in a Community, he received thousands of letters of congratulation, and his plan was the subject of wide discussion.

Cabet went to England to talk the matter over with his friend, Robert Owen. The latter had planned for a great colony in Texas years previous, and it was probably Owen who directed Cabet to Texas. At any rate, he fell into the hands of a certain Peters Land Company, which induced him to believe that he was purchasing 1,000,000 acres. In fact, only 320-acre tracts were sold, and these were evidently government land located for the colonists. Moreover, to secure them there must be certain improvements made before July 1, 1848, and the colonists were able to make improvements on only 32 half-sections, a total of about 10,000 acres instead of a million. But, worst of all, these were not contiguous, but alternate, the others being retained by the vending company.

The first contingent of Icarians (the exact number is not known) arrived in New Orleans, made their way to Shreveport by boat, and then marched overland 250 miles through forests and swamps, with only three ox-teams for the distance of 150 miles. It required two months to get to Icaria, where they were met with the disappointing news regarding the land conditions. They began planting crops, but were ignorant of farming on unbroken prairie sod. All took malaria, and four died. The psysician went insane, and one man was killed by lightning. Meanwhile the second advance guard of 19 (it was to have been 1000 or 1500) arrived in the colony and at once advised abandoning the place. This was done, the colonists dividing into three columns for greater safety. Four men died on the way out. When they reached New Orleans they met 400 newly arrived Icarians, fresh from France, and Cabet arrived soon after. Scouts were sent out for a new location, and finally 250 followed Cabet to Nauvoo, Illinois, where the Mormons had just moved out, leaving the town with only about 4000 inhabitants and with plenty of houses available.

The Icarians prospered on the rented land they cultivated. They established shops and schools and a newspaper. Their numbers increased to 500 by fresh arrivals from France. They had a musical organization with 50 instruments.

Cabet had been made dictator for 10 years, but in 1850 he had surrendered, voluntarily, his powers to a Board of six directors, called the Committee of Gerance, three of whom were chosen every six months, the term of office being a year. Cabet was elected president annually until 1855. In December of that year he proposed that the constitution be revised so as to permit a four years' presidency, with power to name and remove all the subordinate officers of the Community. Cabet said this was necessary for the good government of Icaria and to restore the observation and practice of its principles to those who had departed from them. The proposal to revise prior to March, 1857 was illegal, but Cabet insisted on the change being made at once, regardless of this fact. A compromise was arrived at whereby the regularly-elected president resigned, Cabet taking his place.

For a time Cabet was supported by a majority of the directors, with the General Assembly, to which the directors were subordinate, opposed to him. At the next election, the Board was divided, with the Cabet party in the minority. The latter party quit work, and the two factions were divided throughout the colony in every way. This deplorable condition continued for three months, when the majority party assigned all persons to certain tasks, with the "no work no eat" penalty. Cabet and his party petitioned the State legislature to repeal the act incorporating the colony, determined to ruin if he could not rule. Formal charges were made against the deposed leader, and he was expelled from membership, expelled from the community to which he had given so much of his ability and time. However, 170 remained faithful to him. Four weeks later they were in St. Louis, and a week later Cabet was dead.

The author of "A Brief History of Icaria" says: "The most sensible members of both parties recognize that there were faults on both sides." Cabet had tried to set aside the constitution which he had himself prepared and had tried to arrogate to himself dictatorial powers; but he probably had convinced himself that it was for the best interests of Icaria.

THE CHELTENHAM COMMUNITY — (1858—1864)

Those who went with Cabet did not give up their ideals. Many of them found employment in St. Louis. They began publishing their paper again and kept up some of the life of the colony, especially the social life. Cabet had tried to get them to give up the use of tobacco, and now these faithful ones did. They devoted Sundays to Christian instruction. In 1858 they purchased 28 acres of land for $25,000, about 6 miles from St. Louis. There were some buildings on the place. They reorganized their community life, especially the social life. But again dissensions rent them, the same problems of democratic or more centralized government being the bone of contention. Finally 42 left, and from that time the community declined in every way, until in 1864 there were but 8 left, and they had soon to abandon the project.

THE FIRST IOWA COMMUNITY

The Nauvoo majority, remaining after the first split, numbered about 250 members. They did not prosper, and in 1857 decided to sell their property, or turn it over to creditors, and join the Iowa community. This was finally accomplished in 1860. But they were still not prosperous. Members were leaving, the land was mortgaged, and in 1863 they had but thirty five members. The region was new and uninhabited. Their mortgage drew 10 per cent interest. The labor was hard and unremunerative. But the Civil War enhanced land values and products. They sold 2000 acres for $10,000, reducing their land debt to $5,500. Members began to come back and an era of prosperity set in. They put out orchards and vineyards and built houses. In 1876 when Mr. Hinds visited them, the Icarians had over 2000 acres of fertile land, 700 of it under cultivation, some timber land, much pasture, 600 sheep, 140 cattle, 5 acres potatoes, 5 acres of sorghum, 100 acres of wheat, 250 acres of corn, 1½ acres of strawberries, besides vineyards and orchards. Its property was valued at $60,000 with only

$4000 of debt. Its membership had doubled in the previous ten years.

The population at this time was 83, and fifty applications for membership were pending. Applicants were required to pass a novitiate of six months and were admitted by a vote of three fourths of the membership; seventeen members were admitted in 1876.

The officers of the association were a Director of Agriculture, Director of Industry, Director of Clothing and Lodging, Secretary, Treasurer, and President. All were elected annually, subject to recall at any time. The officers were elected to execute the decisions of the General Assembly and had no other power. Marriage was obligatory. Transgressors were punished by public censure. Women were allowed to take part in the deliberations of the Assembly and to offer propositions, but not to vote.

Trouble arose in 1876, one party wishing to proceed cautiously, the other wishing to hasten improvements, believing the time had come to do so. The latter group was made up of new members and young people who had grown up in the colony. It became known as the Young Party. The struggle became bitter, and finally the split was positive. The Young Party withdrew, taking the matter into the courts, which annulled the charter. Three trustees were appointed by the court to settle up affairs, but were replaced some months later by a committee selected by the Icarians themselves.

In the division of the estate, years of service were taken into consideration, service from the age of sixteen, with no discrimination between sexes. In 1879 the division was made, the Young Party taking the old site, paying a bonus of $1500 for it, the elders moving to a new one which they called the New Icarian Community, on the Nodaway river.

THE YOUNG PARTY

was incorporated for $100,000 with a charter permitting widespread activities. All property was donated by the members to the community, the division having given it to individuals. This agreement of donation provided that it should never be divided between individual members under any circumstances; but, in case of dissolution should go to any number of Icarians who might reorganize to carry out the objects of the association. They adopted an elaborate constitution extending rights of suffrage to women, and the executive government was placed in the hands of four trustees; but the legislative power was held by the General Assembly composed of all persons over 20. They reaffirmed the ideals of the community. A committee of propaganda was appointed and the population of the community was nearly doubled in two months, so that 200 were expected to be reached within the year. Industries were established and agricultural methods improved. There was new zeal and enthusiasm.

But in 1881 another split occurred, and another community was attempted in California at Cloverdale, Sonoma County, the founders being

Adam Dehay and Pierre and Jules Leroux. It grew to have 54 members, 885 acres of land, and $54,000 in capital. But this fourth Icarian community did not make a definite agreement with the parent Young Icarian Community and finally both the California and the Iowa Communities got into trouble, and when the estate was closed up after the property was sold at a sacrifice, the proceeds were divided among the members.

The Young Icarian Community soon broke up, though without lawsuits, and the property was peaceably divided among the members, who were disheartened by the turn that the California affairs had taken.

THE NEW ICARIAN COMMUNITY

began again to rebuild its community life, modeling it very much after the one they had just left. It was successful, though it made no attempt to increase membership, and in 1883 it had thirty-four members, contented, peaceful, and harmonious. The old ways had proven best after all. However, the members were becoming old, and no one of them was willing to take the responsibility of management; so in 1895 the community dissolved by consent of all. But all of the twenty-one remaining members were left in comfortable circumstances. They reluctantly left community life, but were unable to continue it without new members, and were unwilling to take in any new ones.

AN IOWA HISTORIAN'S VERSION OF ICARIA

We are indebted to "The Palimpsest," published by the State Historical Society of Iowa, for the following excerpts from an article by Ruth A. Gallaher, published in the Palimpsest in April, 1921.

"Let us visit Nauvoo again six years later and observe the work of the Communists. In the vicinity of the temple ruins some 500 of the Icarians are living and working, discussing their principles and their daily tasks in the French tongue. On the square surrounding the ruins of the temple, even the walls of which have now been blown down, are the community buildings of the Icarians. A large two-story building provides a combined dining hall and assembly room, the upper floor being used as apartments. A school building in which the boys and girls are taught separately has been constructed from the stones of the temple; and a workshop, remodeled from the old Mormon arsenal, is also in use. Two infirmaries, a pharmacy, a community kitchen, a bakery, a laundry, and a library provide for the welfare of the community. Several hundred acres of land on the outskirts of Nauvoo are farmed by the communists, while the men who are not occupied in farming work in the flour mill, distillery, and saw mill, or are busy in the workshops at tailoring, shoemaking, or other trades, each group choosing its own overseer. The women, with a few exceptions, work in the kitchen, laundry, or sewing rooms.

"Each family has its own apartment, for marriage and the family relation are recognized and fostered. Suppose we observe the life of a family for a day. There is no kitchen in these homes, and the mother does not get the breakfast for the family: instead, all go to the community dining room, where the meal for all has been prepared by the women assigned to this work. After breakfast the father goes to the farm, to the mill, or to the workshop. The mother perhaps washes the dishes or prepares the vegetables for dinner. The boys and girls are sent to school, where they are taught the usual branches and, in addition, the principles of Icaria — all, of course, in French. At noon they again assemble in the dining hall where a dinner of meat, vegetables and fruit is served; then, after a rest, they return to the farm or the shop until the signal calls them to supper. In the evening there may be a meeting to discuss and decide the policies of the community, or the young people may dance. Possibly they may visit together until they are ready to return to their separate homes. On Sundays all unnecessary work is suspended, but there are no religious services.

"If you are of a legal turn of mind and wish to know the political and legal status of these French settlers, you find that the society has a constitution — largely the plan of Cabet — which regulates their domestic affairs. The decisions within the community are settled in the general assembly in which all are expected to be present, although only men over twenty years of age may vote. The relation of the community to the State of Illinois is determined by the act of February 1, 1851, incorporating the 'Icarian Community.' Among the names of the incorporators you may observe one well-known in Iowa and Illinois, A. Piquenard, the architect of the capitol buildings at Des Moines and Springfield. Although jealously maintaining their French language and customs, the men of the community are for the most part naturalized citizens of the United States, and their relations with their American neighbors are usually friendly.

"One faction represented by some fifty-four voters supports Cabet in his attempt to revise the 'constitution and resume his former position of dictator; the other, with eighty-one votes in the assembly, but without much power among the administrative staff, opposes this revision as illegal. This party is known as the "reds." Supporters of Cabet are "whites," "cabetistes," or "furets."

"Fricton is increased by the social groups which have developed among the women and by the class feeling which has appeared among the various groups of workers. The men who work at a distance complain that those who work near the dining hall are served first and receive the best food. All these currents of discontent swell the tide which seems about to engulf the community. Families are divided and men and women on opposite sides no longer speak except when work demands it. In the dining room are tables of the 'reds' and tables of 'cabetistes.'

"Finally the majority party obtain control of the 'gerance' or governing board as well as of the-assembly. Thereupon the 'cabetistes' quit work. Their opponents, taking as their authority the words of Saint Paul — which appeared in French, by Cabet's orders, on the walls of the dining hall — 'If any will not work, neither let him eat,' notified the insurgents that unless they returned to work, food, clothing, and lodging would be refused them. Then, says a French writer, began Homeric battles around the tables as the 'cabetistes' attempted to force their way into the dining hall, to the great damage of the Icarian table ware. Cabet, watching from his room on the second floor, encourages his adherents; but they are finally ousted. A fist fight occurs when the new officials attempt to secure the records and keys from the old administration, while Cabet looks on with a smile, a situation which reminds an Icarian woman — in the opposition, of course — of Charles IX at Saint Bartholomew. The climax of absurdity is reached when the new authorities attempt to remove two women 'cabetistes' who teach in the school for girls. One of the teachers resists and is dragged out 'by the hair' crying for help, while the terrified little girls scream and weep and some neutral American neighbors watch the scene from the vantage point of the temple ruins.

"Again and again the sheriff is summoned to restore order. The mayor of Nauvoo urges a complete separation; and the followers of Cabet withdrew to lodgings outside Icarian jurisdiction and soon after departed for St. Louis, leaving the 'reds' in possession of Icaria.

"What of the group left behind at Nauvoo? Suppose we visit them some twenty years later. To do this we must travel to a spot some four miles east of Corning, Iowa. Here is Icaria, a little hamlet built on a hill sloping down to the Nodaway river. In the center of a square is the dining hall which serves also as the assembly room. On the sides of this square are rows of small white cottages and the shops, laundry, bakery, and similar establishments. Beyond are some log cabins, still used by those for whom frame cottages have not yet been provided. On the outskirts are the barns, gardens, and orchards, while a magnificent wood forms an effective background for the whole. One feature of the usual Iowa village, however, is lacking—no church spire breaks the sky-line above Icaria.

"At Nauvoo the French had found plenty of houses, cultivated fields, and neighbors who were friendly as soon as the suspicion resulting from the struggle with the Mormons was allayed. In Iowa log houses, some without floors or windows, were their only shelter against the biting cold of winter. Most of their land was unfenced and unbroken prairie, and there was not a settler along the trail for forty miles before they reached Icaria. Supplies had to be hauled some hundred miles by team.

"At first they endured real hardships. Only the sick had white bread, sugar, and coffee. Milk, butter, corn bread, and bacon formed the menu of the others. Little by little conditions improved. With the outbreak of the Civil War, the price of wool soared. The Icarians had a large number of sheep and wool was easy to transport to a distant market. Troops passing from the Missouri to the Des Moines river and emigrants westward bound paid generously for supplies. The war, however, was not entirely an advantage; for it is said that every Icarian man qualified to enlist was enrolled in the Union army.

"Each morning they assemble in the common dining room for breakfast of porridge, bread and butter, and coffee. For dinner and supper, meat, vegetables, marmalade, cheese, and fruit may be served. The tables are without cloth, and the members drink from tin-cups. Wine is produced only in sufficient quantities for solemn occasions. Water is the usual drink; and even this indispensible commodity has to be hauled from a distance. Many of the men smoke, but tobacco is not furnished by the community — each smoker must raise and cure his own supply in his leisure hours.

"If you knock at one of the family apartments, you will be received with the courtesy which a French man or woman seldom loses no matter how rough the surroundings. Below are two rooms — a living room and a bed room. Upstairs, close under the roof are two small rooms for the children.

"In the evening when the community assembles in the dining hall for discussion or to enjoy music, a program, or a play, some idea of the personnel at this time may be obtained. Gathered in this rather bare room are some sixty-seven persons, twenty-four of whom are voters. Their dress is plain, but neither peculiar nor standardized * * * "

Of the schism which resulted in a court decree in August, 1878, dissolving the community and causing it to be re-incorporated in two distinct groups, the Iowa author has this to say:

"The property having been divided on the basis of the number of members and the contribution of each in goods and work, the two factions prepared to set up housekeeping anew. The radicals, more aggressive than their opponents, took out a charter under the title, 'La Communaute Icarienne,' taking care to secure all the rights which had been held illegal under the old charter, such as establishing schools and manufacturing establishments. They adopted a program which might have been expressed by the modern slogan, 'Watch us grow,' framed a new constitution, increased their agricultural and industrial activities, gave women a vote in the assembly, and provided for the admission of new members. Apparently they were not very discriminating; for one member wrote in disgust that they had free-lovers, Shakers, nihilists, anarchists, socialists, and cranks of all kinds— the word 'crank' being one of the American words adopted by the French Icarians.

"The result was membership indigestion, and it soon became evident that the community was losing members faster than it gained them. Why was this? the leaders asked in dismay. Some said the withdrawals were due to an instinct similar to that which makes rats leave a sinking ship. This diagnosis was not far wrong. The community was receiving many improvised Icarians who expected to live at ease far from the degrading 'wage slavery' of the cities; and they were both unable and unwilling to cut down trees, build houses, or plough the soil which was exasperatingly full of rocks. Moreover, their families also had to be supported; and the arrival of two skilled mechanics added to the ration list nine additional persons who, a French writer says, had lost none of their Alsatian appetites in the severe climate of Iowa.

"In the meantime, on the bank of the Nodaway, the old Icarians, who had lost both the Icarian name and the village of Icaria, after some hesitation, had incorporated as 'La Nouvelle Communaute Icarienne.' Thus the old Icarians became the new Icarians. They selected a spot about a mile southeast of their old home and created a second Icaria. Here they lived in peace for another twenty years.

"About ten years after the schism six of the nine men in the 'Nouvelle Communaute Icarienne' were over sixty-one years of age. One of these, A. A. Marchand, had been with the first advance guard in 1848.

"As the years passed, the maintenance of the community grew more and more difficult for these old people, and it became evident to even its most devoted adherents that its days were numbered. The final act of the Icarian community as a whole was the vote on the dissolution of the society in February, 1895. The hearts of those who had toiled and suffered in Texas, at Nauvoo, and on the prairies of Iowa must have been heavy, but the vote was unanimous. The execution of the sentence devolved upon the court which appointed E. F. Bettannier, one of the members, receiver. The assets were distributed among the members according to their years of service in the community, reckoning from the age of twenty-one in the case of men and eighteen for the women. Each orphan minor was given $850. Three years later, on the 22nd of October, Judge H. M. Towner accepted the report of the receiver and declared 'La Nouvelle Communaute Icarienne' legally at an end. Some of the members remained as honored citizens in the vicinity, but the last branch of the Icarian tree, which was to have flourished and scattered its seeds into the world of individualism, was dead."

Counting all, this was the seventh Icarian Community, or the fifth not counting the Texas failure or the California hybrid (which permitted private as well as community property). It terminated 47 years of propaganda and effort.

The Icarian colonization experiments enduring far longer than any other with no dogmatic basic. Yet it was marked by many inharmonies. The colonies founded on a firm religious basis existed many years with less dissension and with greater prosperity.

It does not justify, however, the conclusion that only the colonies with a religious basis can continue and prosper. Perhaps it might be that only those with a binding, cohesive, central thought can achieve success, but this is also true of business enterprises, of nations, and even of families. A colony which elevated its community life to the same plane that religious groups have done, and which can educate or induce its members to purge themselves of individualism and selfishness as successfully as have those colonies based on a religious concept, will undoubtedly have an equal prospect of success.

We may be justified in the conclusion that it is not the binding force of a religious ideal, but the binding force of an uplifting ideal which begets the same fervor and devotion, that brings success. Perhaps a community without religion, but with the same honesty, unselfishness and freedom from individualism would greatly transcend the successes of those of religious basis, for it might induce a freedom of intellect which would furnish the urge for greater success than has ever before been known, a cohesive co-operation which would not be enthralled by a limiting religion or a dominating personal influence.

However, in analyzing the Icarian Community, sight must not be lost of the fact that the General Assembly was the supreme power. It is not difficult to imagine that the people were constantly stirred by exhorters, that troublemakers brought their brews to the public in this way, and that local politicians within the group made much hay while the Assembly sun shed its rays upon them. A General Assembly is in theory a gathering of ideas and a presentation of them from which the best may be selected, but in practice it is a chaotic body of irresponsible individuals, each trying to foist his own idea on the group; it is a gathering in which passions rise and the atmosphere becomes tense, and in which bickering and complaining take up most of the time. It is an effort to make calm, dispassionate, unprejudiced, and intelligent legislators out of the entire public, something manifestly impossible. It is difficult to conceive of anything which could more certainly and continuously distract attention from the things which make progress and center them on non-essentials than the General Assembly, that misplaced notion of pure democracy.

We are perhaps not warranted in attributing the downfall of the Icarians to this institution, but we may well note the significant fact that no other group suffered such constant irritation and so many splits. No other institution offers such a fertile field for the airing of minor complaints which may swell into great ones, to create a schism which is irreparable, to scatter suspicion and sow the seeds of dissension. Never was such an opportunity for the spy and the trouble maker, plausible visionaries, and covetous politicians. If Icaria did not suffer more from its form of government than from all other causes combined, we may at least reasonably conclude that no small part of its troubles were probably planned in private and fomented in public, the General Assembly being the means of causing ruptures which resulted seriously, ultimately fatally, for the Icarians.

THE WOMEN'S COMMONWEALTH
1876—1906 (?)

One of the most extraordinary community enterprises ever launched, and one which achieved a high degree of success against seemingly insuperable obstacles that tested the perseverence of its members to the utmost, was the Women's Commonwealth, founded in Belton, Texas, by Mrs. Martha McWhirter about 1876. Its value to the general cause of integral co-operation lies chiefly in its example of heroic endeavor and undying purpose. It is a tale of persistence in the face of persecution. Yet it was doomed to ultimate extinction by reason of the very nature of its beliefs. It was celibate, and, though not confined to women, yet it did not attract men.

The ideals were purely religious, and the Community life was forced for reasons of expediency and economy. Yet it shows the efficiency of this sort of living, for the Community became, if not wealthy, at last well-to-do. The "Sanctified Band," as the members were called, were devoted to principle and self-sacrificing to a degree which makes them models if not martyrs to a belief. Their lives were threatened, their houses stoned, and members were dragged from their beds and cruelly beaten by citizens of the town. Yet the time came when they became one of the town's most valuable assets, and it is probably true that the only individuality Belton, Texas, has ever achieved or ever will, is due to these women.

The women took in washing, wove carpets, turned their hands to whatever tasks promised to hold their little community together. Their boarding house became the best hotel in their town, and achieved fame for many miles around. They bought a steam laundry, bought and rented houses. Mrs. McWhirter became a member of the Board of Trade, the only women ever thus honored. When in 1908 the colony moved to Washington, D. C., the entire town begged them to remain.

The founder of this colony died April 20, 1904, at the age of 77. The colony endured for more than 40 years, disbanding only as the members became superannuated. It is valuable as a demonstration of pertinacity of purpose and of the benefits which accrue to a Community group of definite purpose, and possessed of energy and ideals.

TOPOLOBAMPO COLONY
1891—1900

One of the most stupendous experiments in Community Life, and one which, like that of Robert Owen at New Harmony, was swamped by the number of untried colonists who massed themselves in an untried venture, was the Topolobampo Colony, launched by Albert K. Owen, no relative of Robert Owen, however similar their experiences may have been and however disappointing.

Topolobampo—"Hidden Water"—was a magnificent site with fertile soil and a wonderful climate. Owen, in laying out a railroad on the west coast of Mexico, discovered its possibilities, and for fourteen years laid plans for a giant colonization project. He secured a concession for 300,000 acres from the Mexican government, and 10 million acres for a railroad, with other concessions..

Owen's plan was to make it a true Community within the meaning of this term in this book, with all productive wealth and property owned by the Community as a whole. To finance this huge project, the Credit Foncier was organized, a company which was to lay out Pacific City and make it a model of the world's best knowledge in city-building. Its area was equal to that of New York, one third being devoted to public squares. One hundred thousand shares worth $10 each were issued and sold throughout the world.

The actual work was to commence when $150,000 had been realized from sale of stock, and one hundred pioneers carefully selected were to do the first work. But when only $50,000 had been raised, hundreds of unfit people, many of them with families, rushed into the new colony, swamping it by their numbers, bringing hardships and privations, and intensifying all of the problems that similar Communities under the best of circumstances must meet. Two thirds of the newcomers were women and children. No provision had been made for them, and there was not even fresh drinking water immediately available. In February of 1891, there were 330 persons in the colony, and it was not long until this number was doubled. In 1891 a call was sent out urging all adults with $25 above expenses of reaching Topolobampo to go at once to Topolobampo, also to invest in Bonds in the Mexican Western Railroad Company, which was a part of the colony project.

But rival parties intrigued against Owen with the Mexican government, and efforts were made to supplant the Community features with those of capitalism. Sickness, too, was added to the hardships, and discouragement sat heavily on all. Despite all of these things, however, the colonists built an irrigation canal 8 miles long, 100 feet wide, and 15 feet deep, with 8 miles of laterals. It maintained schools and a kindergarten, put up houses, and had a large adobe building for general purposes and industrial uses. Moreover, it organized a social life. Finally changes were made in the concessions which made it impossible to continue the experiment, and Owen is reported to have said: "All of my efforts have brought only sorrow upon those I tried to serve most."

A letter from L. S. Witmer, now of Florida, but for six months a resident of Topolobampo Colony, says:

"A. K. Owen was the founder of this colony. Owen had something to do along the west coast of Mexico in the 80's, and he discovered a fine harbor with a fine country back of it. He must have been somewhat of a progressive or a radical, or maybe he was a socialist. It struck him that here would be a fine place to start a colony away from civilization and away from capitalism.

"Owen got busy right away and got some very important concessions from the Mexican government. He soon got people in the states interested in the country and his scheme and they went there and founded a settlement along the Fuerta river 30 or 40 miles back from the coast and where they could get some land to irrigate without much expense. When more people came in, they formed another settlement on the coast at the harbor.

"Owen and others got some pretty big ideas in their heads along about this time. They organized a stock company called the Credit Foncier, shares $10 each. A share constituted a membership.

"Getting a big body of land was the first thing this company had to do. They got some Kansas folks interested and they organized a land-holding company called the Kansas-Sinoloa Investment Company. Many thousands of acres of land was secured. The land was very cheap, from a few cents to a few dollars an acre. The next move was to construct an irrigating ditch and build a railroad. The Kansas company undertook the job of digging the ditch, which was to cost around $100,000. The investors got script—$2.00 in script for $1.00 in cash. Bonds or stock was issued to build the railroad. There were four kinds of investments—Credit Foncier stock, railroad bonds, script, and land certificates. The latter were to pay for the land held by the land-holding company.

"Work began on the railroad at once, but it was slow, very slow. The Kansas company took hold of the ditch work and put it thru pretty rapidly. When I was there in the winter of 1891-92, there was a little work done on the railroad, but the ditch was about half done. A customhouse was being built also, and there was some surveying and clearing land. The garden at the river was enlarged and many vegetables were grown. There were men at work all of the time fishing and gathering in clams, duck eggs, turtles, etc.

"We got $3 a day in credits when he worked for the Credit Foncier and $3 a day in script when he worked on the ditch. The credits and the script would buy the necessary things at the commissary, but luxuries had to be paid for in cash. You could get your meals at the big kitchen and dining room, payable in credits or script.

"People lived in tents and temporary structures. Many lived almost the same as out of doors with nothing but a covering overhead. I lived this way for months until I caught the grip and was down and out for months. There was too much exposure and carelessness in the way of living. At times there was much sickness on account of it. Both the companies and the individuals were to blame for this.

"The men who started this colony were surely wise people and they did many wise things. The location, the harbor, the back country, the climate, the ditch, the railroad, and the purchasing of the land were all good—very good. The bad things were the exposure, the housing, the sickness, and the deaths. But the companies were not all to blame for this.

"The people complained and growled and grumbled all of the time and this grew worse and worse until there was a split. After that few people and little money came and not much could be done. Then the two companies went to fighting each other and finally went to law. When I wrote to them about my investments, they said I should not look for anything. 'It may take it all to see the suit through,' they wrote."

A letter from r. M. Campbell, of Los Angeles, written in July, 1924, says:

"In the year 1886, a co-operative colony was organized to carry out the ideals set forth in a book entitled 'Integral Co-operation' by Albert K. Owen and published by John W. Lovell, of New York City.

"This book, picturing the future of co-operation, and the possibilities of this particular location in the State of Sinaloa, Mexico, with its natural deep water harbor on the Gulf of California, its valuable R. R. concession from the government of Mexico, its fertile lands, a valuable option on 100,000 acres, and sundry other attractive features, caused a wide circulation of the book, Integral Co-operation.

"From every state in the union, letters from intensely interested people flooded the N. Y. office and a conference was arranged for all who could be present. The movement was inaugurated by organizing a corporation known as the 'Credit Foncier' of Sinaloa (meaning credit based on our homes). The option on the land was satisfactorily adjusted. A favorable letter from President Diaz was at hand regarding the R. R. concession, and propaganda in the way of a monthly paper was launched.

"Stock subscriptions soon came in to the amount of $100,000.00, and everything indicated an enthusiastic and early beginning of the colony. These were busy days at the colony headquarters in New York and at the branch office in Chicago. The enthusiasm and interest of the California members exceeded their good judgment. They organized a party, chartered a sailing vessel, and made their way to the colony site. It was an ideal location, but it was absolutely undeveloped and barren at the time. Their food supply soon ran short, and the radical change of climate together with contagion, soon caused sickness and death of a few members of this party.

"No plans had yet been made at Headquarters for taking care of the colonists on their arrival, and this move of the California members was unfortunate to say the least. Exaggerated reports were soon "broadcasted" by the newspapers glad of an opportunity to knock the so-called 'Socialist colony' which it was not. Other unorganized parties from other states continued to arrive at the colony in spite of the strenuous efforts at Headquarters to head them off. This did not improve matters at all.

"It was finally arranged to send the first authorized party from Chicago. This party of approximately 25 people including some of the directors and the writer of this narrative, went from Chicago by railway to Guaymas, and upon arrival at the colony set about creating order out of chaotic conditions. Our troubles continued for some time. Internal dissention, fever, and smallpox soon decimated the ranks, although a considerable number have made their homes there since.

"One irrigating canal 7 miles long was built, and to-day the land is devoted largely to the raising of garden truck by private ownership. An immense production of tomatoes is shipped to the states from that section. Of course the colony was a failure from a number of causes. The time was not ripe, and human-nature was child-like, as it is to-day. Altho a failure, it was still a wonderful experience, and many valuable lessons for those planning on similar enterprises can be drawn from this unsuccessful effort in paving the way for the Co-operative Commonwealth.

"The thrilling details of this daring venture are being written up in book form in the hope of their being published, probably by the United Co-operative Industries, and those of the survivors who have intimate knowledge of this enterprise are invited to communicate with Frank M. Campbell, United Co-operative Industries, 11381 Belvedere St., Los Angeles."

Accounts varied so much, according to Hinds, that it was impossible for him to decide what conditions actually were. He shrewdly says: "In large colonies there are generally a few (sometimes many) malcontents, who can see little but evil in the circumstances surrounding them, while to others all is (rose-colored). Most accounts, for instance, of Topolobampo make it the abode of calamity and desolation, especially during the last years, but other accounts represent that colony life, even in that remote region and under its most trying conditions, still had some attractions and compensations, and I have no doubt that many who spent their all to engage in the Topolobampo experiment will be ready to take part in another one should the opportunity offer under conditions apparently more promising of success."

How correct Mr. Hinds was in his surmise is evidenced by the fact that at least two members of the Llano Co-operative Colony lived in Topolobampo and their recollections of it are far from bitter.

In summing up this lamentable experiment, which never had a fair opportunity, a writer enumerates, as reported by Hinds, the conditions necessary to success:

1. Previous mutual acquaintance of the majority of the persons designing to become members;

2. Religious unity and earnestness;

3. A capable leader who shall be unanimously accepted as such and obeyed;

4. Some actual training in giving and receiving personal criticism;

5. A sober calculation as to the means of earning a livihood. This should include care in the selection of a location.

Yet not all of these are absolutely essential, however desirable they may be. Strong leadership is necessary at the inception, but it may eventually become a weakness rather than a source of strength, as many examples show. Previous acquaintance is not necessary, nor is it any guarantee that such previously acquainted individuals will retain their friendships when put to the test of colony conditions. Earnestness of purpose is imperative to success, just as it is to the success of any undertaking; but it remains to be proven that religious unity is essential; if there be no conflicting forms of militant religion, mere religious tolerance is sufficient, if we are to believe the examples given of communities which have lived for many years with religious tolerance. A sober calculation as to the means of earning a livlihood and the selection of a location are surely necessary. Actual training in giving and receiving mutual criticism is valuable; mutual criticism is inevitable, and those who cannot bear it will not remain with any Community.

THE RUSKIN COMMONWEALTH
1894-1901

J. A. Wayland, who became well known as the editor and owner of the Appeal to Reason, the fighting Socialist paper, founded the Ruskin Colony in 1894. He was publisher of the Coming Nation, and agreed with his readers that if the circulation were pushed to 100,000 he would use $23,-000 to purchase land on which a colony should be established to demonstrate the theories espoused by the paper. Charter memberships were $500. The first location was found unsuited for the purpose, but eventually a good location was secured.

The chief industry was publishing the Coming Nation, and the printery was a good one. At one time a publisher of a string of labor papers made arrangements to have them printed at the colony printing establishment. However, discords early set in, and Wayland withdrew at the end of a year, selling his publication to the colony. Steady progress was made by the colony, however, until in 1899. On July 26 of that year the entire property was disposed of at forced sale. It consisted of 1700 acres of land, many buildings, 200 acres of growing crops, 184 head of live stock, poultry, merchandise, machinery, and tools.

The trouble was caused by the rule-or-ruin methods of self-seekers, as has been the case in other communities not under the leadership of a firm character and one in whom all members have confidence. Ruskin was purely secular, and there was none of the cohesive force given by a religious ideal upon which all agree. It seems to have tried to combine to some extent the Community principles with some individual undertakings.

Notwithstanding that the rule-or-ruin members resorted to injunctions and caused the premature failure of the colony, its assets were more than its liabilities, even in the face of a forced sale, and there was a surplus to divide among members.

About 250 Ruskin members went to Duke, Georgia, after the failure of the Tennessee effort, and made another attempt. A special train of 11 cars was chartered at a cost of $3500, and the household goods and other belongings, including tools, type, the press of the Coming Nation, and other equipment were shipped. They were joined by 35 other members, and the new Ruskin Commonwealth, established by the Co-operative Settlers' Association, had 800 acres of land, an abundance of timber, more than 50 houses, a postoffice, store, railroad station, and siding. The publication of the Coming Nation was resumed and various business enterprises started, among them being the making of shingles, brooms, cereal coffee, leather suspenders. Fruit-growing and poultry-raising were established. Social life flourished too, and there was a Woman's Club, a lyceum, theatrical entertainments, brass band, and other musical organizations.

However, the same dissension entered and the outcome was the same. Some left for the Fairhope Single-Tax Colony, some went back to Tennessee. In 1901 a final disposition of the colony's effects was made, and the chapter was closed.

The weakness of both the Ruskin experiments seems to have been a lack of a common community interest entirely divorced from selfish interests, and the lack of calm and dispassionate leadership. Its importance was not great, but J. A. Wawland was forever convinced that Community life is impossible except in religious colonies; and the Appeal to Reason frequently printed an article warning against such enterprises. This was to do much toward deterring people from joining the Llano Co-operative Colony when the latter was formed in 1914. Great stress was laid on the purely material features of colony life and the individual benefits to be enjoyed. This made an appeal to selfishness which is the common weakness of secular communities. Religious colonies usually escape this; for their communal living is filled with a burning enthusiasm for a principle for which they are ready to sacrifice all. Secular colonies are rarely animated by such high ideals.

THE CHRISTIAN COMMONWEALTH
1896—1900

Not all religious colonies succeed, however. Christian Commonwealth of Muscogee County, Georgia was launched in 1896 by Rev. Ralph Albertson, with 45 persons as the nucleus. During its existence 500 persons were connected with it first and last. It printed a paper which attained a circulation of 2000, had a library of 1400 volumes; it had a sawmill, shops, cotton mill, printing establishment, laundry, and school house, and all rough buildings. There was night school three evenings a week for elders, and a kindergarten for infants. Women had equal rights with men, and the majority ruled in the colony.

The chief weakness of this colony—and one which merits its presentation in the pages of this little volume — was the child-like determination to open the doors to all comers. The kind-hearted founders objected especially to excluding the weak and needy, and ignored all the usual requirements in regard to age, health, and membership fees. This was a splendid idealism, but it was not likely to bring in substantial material on which to build a colony, and neither was it likely to sift out those who were unable to comprehend the high principles of the leaders.

Though the reasons for failure given by Rev. Albertson were a $2000 mortgage and poor land with crop failures, Hinds sums it up quite differently; and his analysis is that "it still would not have been in existence to-day unless radical changes had taken place in its regulations regarding the admission of members. No Community that has thrown wide open its doors to all applicants has long survived. No wonder it had to expel one member for immoral tendencies, one for incurable laziness, and one for making false statements about his family! No wonder there came in those who kept away from religious meetings, mocked at prayer, trampled on their vows, set aside their contracts, and who were determined to rule or ruin and finally, after making up their minds to leave the colony, applied for a receivership in order to break it up and thereby secure a part of the common property! Its founders and leaders may not have banked too largely on Christ's love, but He was remarkable also for his prudence and foresight and cautioned his disciples against giving 'that which is holy unto dogs' and casting 'pearls before swine.' "

The achievements of this little group were not momentous, but the lesson to be learned from allowing a love for humanity to mistakenly admit those who are manifestly unfit for Community life is too plain to be overlooked. Things which are given away too freely are likely to be lightly valued, and the colony which makes too easy the terms of admittance into full membership is "casting its pearls before swine."

THE BROTHERHOOD CO-OPERATIVE COMMUNITY OF EQUALITY
1898—1906

This rather long title is usually cut down to Equality, which was organized in 1895 by Socialists and officials of the Socialist organization. It found favor with the delegates to a Socialist convention in 1898, and in that year a call was sent out to Socialists to go to Puget Sound. The organization had a membership of 3,000 paying ten cents a month.

In October of 1900 the colony had stated the population to be 120; in 1898 it had been given at 260 to 300. One authority claims that 300 persons left during the first 18 months for various reasons. This is believable; many who go into new enterprises, whether Community or otherwise, are very unfit for the conditions they must meet. Those who take up government land rarely carry their holdings thru to the time when they really produce. Newly opened districts change populations frequently. Communities have no monopoly on this. It is only the common interest that makes this turn-over in population seem to be more important than in other cases, and perhaps it is more important.

Equality was a real Community in the ownership of property, and in sharing earnings all over 18 were on equality.

In 1900 the colony had 620 acres of land, with 35 of them under cultivation. In 1901 it showed resources of $75,000; its liabilities were only $1,000.

Causes of disintegration and final failure are attributed by Hinds to various incidents. There were no recognized leaders, though J. E. Pelton was the chief one until his death. There were many disputes, and in 1904 there was a disastrous fire which cost the colony $8,000. The General Assembly seems to have been the controlling factor, and to have been the same costly institution there that it was in the other colonies. So bad did conditions become, according to an article in SUNSET in 1923, that fist-fights were common in the Assembly, and it was claimed by some that buildings were burned by contending factions. A letter received some years ago by the compiler of this little volume from a former member of Equality stated that "we burned the barn." An effort was made to get more definite information; but the reply to the letter sent out brought the statement from a younger relative that the old colonist had become irresponsible in his old age and that there was no truth in his assertion. The Llano Colony had several former members of Equality at one time. All were much in evidence at the Llano General Assembly, and the threat was made that some might take such violent measures as were taken in Equality, though this assertion was not traced to them.

48

Several accounts of the final failure of the Colony seem to lay much of this to Alexander Horr, who came to Equality in 1904. Horr induced about forty of the remaining colonists, virtually all of them, to adopt the plans of Theodore Hertzka, by which they divided into groups. This plan is known as "free competition," and when the compiler of this book met Horr in San Francisco in 1922, just before Horr was nominated as candidate for governor on the Socialist party ticket, the latter was still advocating the Hertzka plan and was much opposed to Community life. Briefly, this plan is for the colony to advance funds to groups to engage in industry. Free competition is guaranteed, as the workers can join whatever groups suit them. But as profits are divided within the groups, the desire will be to join those making the greatest profits, so that, as in ordinary capitalistic competitive society, the tendency will be toward an equality. Horr and two other trustees pushed through a scheme of this kind, notwithstanding some opposition, and leased to themselves 160 acres of colony land for 99 years. The majority obtained an injunction against Horr and finally a receiver was appointed in March, 1916.

A second colony had previously been established at Edison as a part of the chain of colonies which was to be formed, but it did not survive long.

Wm. Lieseke writes from Langley, Washington regarding Equality Colony, on April 10, 1924, as follows:

" * * * I will say a big part of the members of the colony when I was there didn't claim to be Socialists and surely didn't prove it. About 140 people were in the colony when I was and, coming and going, we held our own. I worked three months in the cuisine as superintendent, and all the time I worked in that position I came in contact with all of the members daily. I could have picked out 50 good co-operators of the bunch, but we had no leader and had a strong following of the trouble-makers, and I must say here that he was much to blame for much of the trouble we had when I was there, and I suppose he kept on after we left. I will not go into details; let us forget it. * * * Had a letter from X—still knocking Llano. Told me not to send money there, as it is a lost proposition. Too bad, but then we can't blame him; he doesn't know any better."

Mr. Lieseke's observations regarding a certain member who continued to make trouble, and who, to the knowledge of the writer, was in at least two colonies subsequently, seems to confirm the theory that there is a type of people who cannot refrain from making trouble, and who seem to seek trouble. They are well characterized by G. J. Holyoake in commenting on the struggles of the Rochdale Co-operators, given on another page of this book.

It is not difficult to understand that the pioneers of Equality, those with ideals and vision and honest intentions and some degree of practicality were greatly handicapped by those who were in the colony purely for personal gain. It is this fact which has given religious colonies success, where failure has attended the efforts of secular organizations. Lacking a strong leader, and loaded down with persons who sought only advantages for themselves, with the good of the community second in their thoughts, if indeed it occupied any place whatsoever, it required no court decree to bring about failure. The death of the colony was decreed by the selfish attitude of the majority members.

Worth Wilson Caldwell, writing in the Bellingham Sunday Reveille in October, 1922, says: " * * * The facts prove that they (the Equality Colony) existed for approximately one third of what it cost the people in the neighboring towns to survive. This was due, of course, to the fact that everything they bought was raw materials and was made up free of charge by the company men * * *. According to survivors of this seemingly happy arrangement, many people came without any real intention of subscribing to the principles of the colony and lived in their midst until they stocked up on a large quantity of extra clothing and so on and then moved away." This fits in very well with what Mr. Lieseke writes, though many accounts written of Equality fail to give all the facts, or else carry many unwarranted assertions, according to Mr. Lieseke.

In summing up the failure of Equality Colony, the shrewd and kindly Mr. Hinds says: "And thus practically ended in strife the experiment that excited at first so much interest and which it was hoped would lead to such large results. Its experience emphasizes anew the lesson taught by the scores of Owenite and Fourierite experiments in the first half of the last century: To rear a durable structure of any sort there must be either selected material or arrangements for changing its character and eliminating the worthless. This is especially true of all structures in which human beings are the material. If such selected material is not obtainable, and there is no suitable machinery for changing the character of the material offered, then it seems the acme of unwisdom to bring men, women, and children into the close relations of colony life. In accounting for the unfortunate results at Equality, it would be difficult to improve upon the statement made by one of its residents in the colony's paper: **"The underlying cause of our troubles has been the indisputable fact that as Socialists most of us were pulled before we were ripe. We thought we had reduced Socialism to a science before we had mastered the alphabet thereof. And, furthermore, we did not analyze our own natures to discover how much of the old competitive, murderous, individualistic spite yet lingered therein."**

COSME COLONY, Paraguay, S. A.
1893—1904

We are indebted to Mr. Fred Harris of Brisbane for clippings from the "Standard" of that city giving a lecture by John Lane, brother of William Lane, concerning the New Australian and Cosme efforts. Mr. Lane gave this lecture in May, 1924, excerpts from which are given here:

I should like you to get in true vision William Lane's idea of the life he was striving for, of the right-living he so earnestly advocated, of the underlying religion which was the basis of all his teachings, whether applied to social reform in Queensland or to social living in Paraguay. I give you his own words:—

"God speaks in the springing of the corn, in the march of the stars, in the movements of peoples, and in the wondrous justice which underlies the pains and pleasures of our lives. Never yet has chaos been; never yet disorder. Never has the wrong really triumphed; never in all the ages has the right really gone down."

* * * * *

"We Germanic peoples come into history as Communists. From our communal villages we drew the strength which broke Rome down, the energy which even yet lets us live. Not where men beg landless for work in electric-lighted factories, not where women, poverty-fearing amid heaps of riches, shrink from child-bearing, was the courage born that still keeps the drum-tap beating with the sun. It was from wife-kept homes in free villages, where the land was common and all were equal, and only the sluggard and the criminal were outcast, where every man had friends to stand by him in his need."

* * * *

William Lane got into close personal touch with the bushworkers during the shearers' strike of '91. Here is his message to them, written in 1892:—

"For this to me is what New Australia means; to the landless, the homeless, the wifeless, the childless; to those whose hearts are sick and sore; to those who long to be manly, to be true, to be what men should be:

"Come out from this hateful life, the life that is full of unspoken misery, of heart-sickening longing, of evil habits growing with the years, of sin and slavery that lead to nothing but death.

"Come together in all unselfishness to trust each other and to be free. To live simply, to work hardly, to win, not the gold that poisons, but the home that saves! To be true husband to one woman, to be happy father of healthy children, to be true friend of every mate who grips hands for the well-being of all!

"Come and work as free men for each other, to labor on the common land for the common good, and not for self alone, or the selfish greed of

&nother!' "

In 1892 William Lane left the "Worker," and devoted some months to organizing for the proposed co-operative colony. Prospectors were sent to South America (Australian governments in those day were bitterly anti-Socialistic), and succeeded in obtaining a large grant of land under settlement conditions in Paraguay.

In July, 1893, the new Australia pioneers set sail for Paraguay.

But, from the first, there was no real unity among the colonists; and when, after some expulsions and many secessions, a second party arrived from Australia only to intensify the differences, it was clear that to build up a communal colony with the material in New Australia was utterly impossible.

In May, 1894, 58 people (39 of them men, and mostly bushmen) under the leadership of William Lane, withdrew from New Australia to begin again the task of building up a communal settlement.

Mr. Gilmore writes: "After William Lane left, first one person was chairman, then another; one arrangement followed another; troubles and dissensions grew; parties formed * * * each one petitioning the Government against the other, till at last that most long-suffering of bodies, the Paraguayan Government, interfered and sent out an official to fix things up and report. The result was, that the colony ceased, in the original sense of the word, to be a colony, the Government giving each settler so many acres of land for his individual use. The Paraguayan and the New Australian live side by side, equal under the law, and equal socially."

On leaving New Australia, we camped near a river ford called Paso

COSME COLONY

Cosme, while our agents tried to secure a grant of land for us from the Government. But a revolution occurred, making an immediate grant impossible, and forcing us, poor though we were, to buy privately.

We secured a block of 13,000 acres in the fork of two rivers, near Caazapa. The price, £400; one quarter cash, and payment of balance within three years. Later on the new Government paid us back our £100 deposit and took up the other payments. We always found the Paraguayan Government most liberal and helpful in their dealings with us.

Cosme started with a capital of less than £400, mainly provided by English and Australian friends, and by the sale of personal effects contributed by members. The women gave their jewelry—even their wedding rings, which last, however, was not sold, but given back to the owners. A soaking rain was falling on that bleak day in July, 1894, when the hired native carettas left us and our belongings in the long wet grass at the edge of that Paraguayan monte, which we were to call home. But, though it soaked our garments, the rain could not damp our spirits, for dissensions were left behind, and we were on our own land. Before nightfall, all were under shelter of some sort; tents, with grass-thatched flys, huts of saplings, with grass roof and sides.

The machete men first cleared the undergrowth. The axemen felled and cut up the timber. Then came the stackers and burners. The planting gang followed on the heels of the burners, with hoe and seed maize over the hot, ash-covered ground, till in a few weeks the extending clearing smiled its green promise of harvest. As the day grew longer our scanty stores grew shorter, till our cash was spent, our food gone, and another month to go before our earliest maize would be ripe for harvest. A Caazapa storekeeper sold us a ton of beans on credit, but during the last fortnight we had no salt to go with them. Then the maize crop came in, and mandioca, sweet potatoes, and more slowly maturing crops in swift succession, and we feasted and enjoyed those simple foods most ambrosially flavored by hard work and much abstinence.

As the weeks passed our Australians tightened their belts and swung their axes. They grew leaner and browner as summer came on, but insisted on the small store of finer foods being shared by women and children only. They were living Sir Philip Sidneys. I know, for I served out the stores. Several became sick with stomach troubles; but they simply would not take the extra and better food which we always managed to reserve for the sick. They smiled and joked through it all and never grumbled.

Whenever my faith in human nature tends to weaken I have only to think of those fine Australians I had the honor to be mates with in those early days of Cosme, and my faith grows strong again. It does one good to find how good poor old human nature is, to know to what great heights it can rise.

Co-operative Labor.—All males over 15 and single women over 16 years of age were on the staff of organized workers. Work was directed by an industrial manager, who received general instructions from the committee. We had a 45-hour week. Work was varied and largely agricultural. All labor was treated as of the same value. Disagreeable work was shared 'round as much as possible.

Communal Owning.—All wealth, excepting purely personal possessions, such as clothing and personal effects, was owned by the community. Land, houses, crops, machinery, tools, stock, and general goods were all communal property. Members had individual use-hold of house and allotment. Such use-hold was of a permanent nature, and did not prevent a man improving his house or growing fruit or flowers in his garden.

Communal Sharing.—All adults had equal shares, irrespective of age, sex, capacity, or occupation. Proportionate shares were given to children according to age. Whenever it could be reasonably and economically done "free issue" was practiced. Thus, certain things easily grown and produced were on the "freelist," and were handed out without limit or charge; i.e., treacle, mandioca, sweet potatoes, bananas, oranges, and tobacco.

Limited supplies of home-grown products were shared 'round equally. Goods bought from outside were supplied on an equal credit system, the effect of which was that all got equal value of this class of goods, but pleased themselves as to the relative proportions of the different articles they took.

Government.—Absolutely democratic, general meeting being the basis of all authority. Colony affairs were managed by a chairman, committee, and an industrial manager, all elected by direct vote of members. The committee met weekly and decided on the general plan of colony business. The industrial manager superintended all industrial affairs, and reported weekly to the committee. The ordinary general meeting of members was held yearly. Special general meetings could be called at any time. Single women had the right to vote, which right, together with its correlative duty—communal labor under the direction of the Cosme authority—they resigned on marriage.

Teetotalism.—The colony was teetotal. Those who joined accepted it as a principle. Few members were abstainers before joining, but the principle was steadfastly adhered to, and Cosme children had never seen a drunken man.

Religion.—In Cosme there was no church, no priest, no ritual, and no recognized religion in the common meaning of the word, implying as it does, belief in certain dogmas and conformity to certain routine observances. But I found Cosme a very religious place; for there religion in its highest sense— the uplifting of man's moral nature in the every-day tendencies of living— was always present.

One of the most noticeable effects of communal living was the constantly rising standard of art as shown in music, drama, and literature. The early concerts tended to crudeness. With few exceptions the items were dreary and the audience bored. But a singing class was formed. Almost everybody tried to join. The toneless and tuneless were weeded out, and singing forged ahead. The dreary, many-versed old-time songs gave way to minstrel melodies with harmonized choruses; then the minstrels developed into glee-singers, and later on into performers in opera and oratorio. Musical folk who could not sing took to instrumental music. The non-musical took to plays. At first the screaming farce was the vogue; then came the Sheridan and Goldsmith comedies, leading up to Shakespeare, the final favorite.

The same growth in appreciation of good literature was just as marked. I remember how in the grass dining-room, a very fine lecture by H. S. Taylor, on "Shelley," sent the bulk of the audience to sleep. But "Evening Notes," with Wm. Lane as editor, and the Sunday evening readings, gleaned from many favorite authors, quickly trained the Cosme ear and mind, and soon made a fine audience for good English. "Evening Notes" also provided a ready outlet and kindly critical hearers for any with the talent for scribbling.

My thoughts even now linger longingly on the social side of Cosme. I have since lived in a social desert cheered by but too few oases. And when one considers that this active healthy social living was attained in so short a time by men and women, mostly of poor education, none highly educated, not one university degree in the whole lot—what must one think of what social life would become if from childhood all would grow up in fitting social environment with talented teachers in the arts which provide such true, deep, and lasting pleasures?

In 1896 the colony having overcome the pioneering difficulties, Wm. Lane went to Britain to organize new members, it being regarded as absolutely necessary to equalize the sexes so as to give the bachelors opportunity to marry. But the primitive housing and surroundings, hot climate, different and coarser food, insect pests, rough and unaccustomed work, together with that general strangeness and newness of things, so often the cause of homesickness among the faint-hearted, all combined to make most of the newcomers dissatisfied with Cosme life and soon to leave it.

This breakdown of our efforts to equalize the sexes was the very natural and reasonable cause of most of our pioneer bachelors leaving. They had joined in the hope and expectation of being able to settle down in homes of their own. Withdrawals owing to hardships steadily decreased as the years went by and the standard of living rose.

But another class of difficulty was always present and only lessened as members adapted themselves to Cosme living. This difficulty was the complete change in the ethics of every-day life, and the consequent necessity of changing one's mode of action toward both the individual and the community, which breaking of lifelong habits, and formation of new ones, made no small call on the patience, forbearance, and persistence of the colonist.

Some left because they found the place too individualistic, more because they felt too keenly "the restraints of Communism." Some found themselves temperamentally unfitted for exercising the quality of forbearance, so very necessary for harmonious life. Several who joined were of the type that can see only one right way of doing anything, whether digging a post-hole or compiling a constitution; and if they were not sound enough democrats to abide loyally by the will of the majority they would get out of touch and drift away. Some bachelors left, intending to return in double harness. Several benedicts departed because their wives never took kindly to a place from which the keen joys of bargain shopping were missing. One elderly lady suffered from orthodox religious views, and felt so unhappy because of the presence of Sunday cricket and the absence of church and parson that her relatives—very good colonists—felt compelled to remove to more pious surroundings. Some went to support aged relatives in England or Australia. Some took strong personal dislikes, and found the place too small, while a few were born nomads and could no more settle down on Cosme than anywhere else.

William Lane left the colony in 1899. He felt he could do more effective work by press writing in the outside world. He also wanted to earn money to liquidate a loan which the colony had received, and for which he regarded himself as personally liable.

In 1901 another effort was made to increase membership. I came to Australia to obtain more members, and no special difficulty was found in getting recruits; but the results turned out to be as before, though this time none left on account of hardships.

In May, 1904, the population was only 69—33 adults and 36 children.

I myself considered that Cosme's only chance of keeping white was to grow. If it failed to grow it must ultimately become Paraguayan. I could not risk that for my children, so I decided to return to Australia. I left Cosme at the end of 1904.

That is almost 20 years ago. I am informed that the colony since then gradually drifted into individualism, and the land and property were divided up among those who remained.

The slogan of Cosme Colony was "Cosme does all it possibly can for its members, and it relies on them to think as much of the colony as they do of themselves, if not a little more."

At the death of William Lane, a brief biography was written in an Australian labor paper by Mr. S. S. Ross:

"Billy Lane is dead—dear old Billy Lane. And he died in the camp of the enemy. There is the infinite tragedy of it * * * It was hard to accept the fact of Lane's death. He was so much to so many of us years ago. Never phrase maker so magical, nor personality so picturesque, nor preacher so magnetic, nor propagandist so mighty to us of the 90's * * * Those who came under his influence were stirred to the depths, mentally and spiritually. He made all things new. * * *

"My memories are rocking and shouting as I think of Billy Lane, of, by, and for the people, man of the mob. soul of the cause, lever of the movement."

"He wrote and he preached and he stormed at the trades unions. He did more. He organized them in preparation for action, infecting, if not the rank and file, those whose services were the more effective, the leading officials of the various branches and trades * * * He showered pamphlets in thousands among them. He had agents in every center of population. His weekly paper circulated in every mining camp and shearing shed in Queensland * * * He founded debating societies and reading clubs * * * His magnetic personality drew hundreds of young workers, artisans, clerks, and many of the restless, discontented enthusiasts in every walk of life around him. He succeeded * * * in establishing the best organized band of workers in Australia, and probably in the world.

"While on the 'Worker,' Lane conceived the star-tinted idea of the New

Australia Co-operative Settlement. Curiously enough, not that so many were drawn into this celebrated experiment in communism, but comparatively a few, is the marvel historians must not forget. Ere long Lane resigned the editorship and devoted his shining talents to organizing recruits for Paraguay, South America. In the yellowing little paper he wrote his captivating best. In 1893 Lane left Queensland never to set foot again on its soil. For six years he labored in "New Australia" and "Cosme," thence returning to Australia an altered and beaten man."

William Lane went back into newspaper work; but he was unable to forget his disappointment, and seemed to strive to obliterate his former personity. Lane died at the age of 56.

From the "Cosme Monthly" of July, 1903, then in the ninth year of publication, we take the following descriptive account of Cosme, written by E. H. Lane.

"We travel to Cosme from the Maciel railway station by carreta (two-wheeled bullock wagon); eight miles brings us to Caazapa, the nearest township to the colony; nine miles more and we reach the Pirago river, which we cross by means of the bridge * * *. This bridge was built some six years ago under the supervision of Allan McLeod, the present industrial manager of the colony. It is of great local benefit, and is indicative of the reasons why the Paraguan government and people are interested in the well-being of Cosme. Another mile takes us over the river estero (flat, semi-swampy land), then, after crossing some open grass land, we enter one of the far-famed montes of Paraguay and pass the Cosme river. Words cannot convey any adequate idea of the beauty of the Paraguayan forest. The road is cut through the very heart of it. Overhead tower the trees, intertwined with huge creepers, making the sky itself but a faint background to the ever-green arch. Timber, altogether strange to the newcomer, is on every side; but palms and many well-remembered species of fern life flourish in wondrous luxuriance. The irrepressible wild orange trees, laden with golden fruit, struggle bravely to pierce the dense foliage and salute the sun, while myriads of parrots and other gaudy birds break the stillness of the pervading calm.

"Originally the Cosmans were living on some open campland * * *. As soon as the monte was cleared, the village was planned and houses were gradually built until the old site was entirely deserted and every one became domiciled in the village. The houses varied in size according to the number in a family, from the one room of the single man to the four-roomed cottage and kitchen of the larger families. The frame and walls of the houses are now built of sawn timber, roofs thatched, earthen floors which are now being improved with wood blocking, no windows (but shutters) yet, for all that, good, weather-proof houses. Each of the houses has enough ground to enable the occupier to follow to the top of his bent any gardening ideas he may have * * *. Many of the gardens are nicely laid out with roses, carnations, violets, honeysuckle, and many other well-known favorites * * *. Fruit trees are planted in the streets, and some also in nearly all the gardens, while ornamental trees are also in evidence * * *.

About 300 yards from the village, in the midst of the vivid green of the sugar cane, are the colony workshops. Here is the center of the community's industrial life. The main building is a fine substantial structure 60 feet long, 40 feet wide, and 24 feet high. It is built of solid and durable timber throughout. Attached to it are the sugar boiling works and smithy. In the workshops are the cane mill, corn mill, sawing plant, carpenters bench, lathes, and morticing machine. The sugar is stored on the top floor, where also is the tobacco press. The machinery is driven by a substantial 14 h.p. steam engine. In the workshops almost every kind of work necessary for the colony is turned out— sugar, corn meal, sawn timber, carts, furniture, iron work, books, and many tools.

Oranges are everywhere, in monte, grove, street, and garden. The golden fruit is ripe and superabundant from May to December and adds a charm to everything. * * * All sorts thrive equally well. Lemons and limes are ripe and plentiful all the year 'round. Close to the village is a grove of 1500 oranges, limes, and lemons; but there is plenty of fruit on the trees in the streets to supply all needs for a couple of months yet * * *"

The population at this time was published as being 30 men, 15 women, and 50 children, a total of 95, with 6 men and two women absent on leave.

Operations recorded consisted of sugar-making, building, fencing, hauling, stock-raising, boot-making, tanning, gardening, teaching, cooking, butchering, storekeeping, printing, and mail-carrying. A financial report in some detail showed funds derived from various sources, including the Paraguayan government.

It advertised for members, but stipulated they must be strong, healthy people able to subscribe to Cosme principles and not afraid of hard work and living. "Full membership is in each case preceded by a year's trial membership in the colony." Membership agents were listed in England and Australia.

A synopsis compiled from material gathered from various sources by an Australian interested in this venture, gives an epitomized history as follows:

Cosme began with 30 pioneers whose capital averaged about $25 a head. They had to clear a dense jungle. Education was primary and the study of literature was always a prominent feature of the Cosme life. The land was originally in the name of the founder, William Lane, who later transferred it to a Board of Trustees. These trustees had to have a resident membership of 5 years. The colony was seven years old when the resident clause came into force. The hours of labor were 45 a week and disagreeable labor was shared by all.

On an average the males outnumbered the females by 2 to 1 in the colony. The industries were tannery, sugar mills, sawmill. * * * Government consisted of a president and committee of three, with one industrial manager elected on adult male franchise. The trustees were nine in number and a two-thirds majority was necessary to make or unmake a rule at any meeting. The meetings were executive, board of trustees, and Annual-Conference. Single men were barred from the colony from time to time because of the preponderance of males over females.

Fires at various times, destroying the social hall, library, tannery, and several dwellings. Nothing was insured. The highest membership was attained in 1895 and was 150; but in 1904 this had dwindled to 65. The absence of modern agricultural machinery was a great drawback at all times * * *. In 1899 the Ruskin Colony of Tennessee was offered a large tract of the Paraguay land by the Cosme colonists. The chief crops and source of income were from sugar cane and lumbering. Money for financing the colony was obtained from a private company, but at high rates of interest. William Lane also loaned money, but this was free from interest.

Any comment on Cosme could be only in admiration of the fortitude and singleness of purpose of those hardy Australians with their high idealism and devotion to principle. They were evidently of the right type, and it was no fault of either them as persons nor of their colony as organized that they failed to succeed, but rather of an unfortunate choice of location.

As Fred Harris comments: '* * * I have often wondered * * * why Lane went to the expense to fit out a full-rigged ship to start in an unknown part of the world, among a people who spoke a different language, and far from their kith and kin, which fact John Lane refers to concerning some of the secessions from Cosme; but probably it was on account of the hostile Tory Government that ruled here at that period. Over here we have climatic conditions equal to anything in the world * * *"

Whatever the reason, it is quite propable, as Mr. John Lane analyzes it, that the remoteness and the difficulty in getting people to be satisfied so far away had much to do with the failure. Yet it was not a failure from material causes, but a breaking down of the colony or community spirit and a slipping into individualism after more than a decade because of the lack of new recruits to keep the community growing. This may reasonably be attributed to its location. Whatever other trials might have beset it had it been in an English-speaking country are problematical, but it seems that we are justified in concluding that Cosme has demonstrated that Community life on a secular basis is possible, and that with a desirable location the chances of success are sufficient to justify such experiments being made. Cosme has contributed to the history of Communities an important chapter. Individualistic communities similarly located have failed in much less time, and their failure has been spiritual as well as material; this was not true of Cosme.

SMALL OR SHORT-LIVED COMMUNITIES

FRUITLANDS

This was a short-lived colony founded at Harvard, Massachusetts, founded at a little later date than Brook Farm. Transcendentalists were the membership. It was organized as a "family." No money was handled by members. They used no animal foods, not even milk or eggs. Neither did they use tea, coffee, molasses, rice, or any thing not grown there. They used pine knots to furnish light. They did not even enslave animals for domestic use, and used the spade instead of the plow. Its life was but a few months, and it is chiefly important in this history because it shows the rather fanatical groups which have tried to associate themselves in Community life, persons so utterly impractical in an enterprise where the utmost practicality is needed, that their early failure is foreshadowed by their fantastic notions.

SKANEATELES COMMUNITY
1844 to 1846

This Community was established in Skaneateles, New York, by John A. Collins, and can be considered the experiment of this one man; for the land was held in his name, chiefly, though another man's name was used in a way which subsequently caused trouble. It was non-religious, but not irreligious. Its location was favorable; it had 300 acres of land, 70 covered with fine timber, the rest fenced, 40 acres of wheat, 130 acres of corn, besides vegetables and fruits and grain. There was a two-story stone house well furnished, with a 30-foot extension, with other buildings. It had water power and a mill with wood-working machinery. The number of colonists was about 90. When the colony was terminated because its founder did not care to go on with it any longer, the property was worth twice what was paid for it. One of the reasons why the founder decided on this may be judged from his characterization of the people who go into colonies. He says:

"Our previous convictions have been confirmed that not all who are most clamorous for reform are competent to become successful agents for its accomplishment—that there is floating upon the surface of society a body of restless, disappointed, jealous, indolent spirits, disgusted with our present social system, not because it enchains the masses to poverty, ignorance, vice, and endless servitude, but because they could not render it subservient to their private ends. Experience convinces us that this class stands ready to mount every new movement that promises ease, abundance, and individual freedom; and that when such an enterprise refuses to interpret license for freedom, and insists that every member shall make his strength, skill, and talent subservient to the movement, then the cry of tyranny and oppression is raised against those who advocate such industry and self-denial—then the enterprise must become a scapegoat, to bear the fickleness, indolence, selfishness, and envy of this class."

There were disturbers at Skaneateles, and they were hired to go. The Community did not expel them, as it had a right to do, but purchased their leaving at a cost of $3,000. And Mr. Collins says: "In this winnowing process it would be remarkable if much good wheat were not carried off with the chaff.

"The problem of social reform must be solved by its own members—by those possessed of living faith, indomitable perseverance, unflinching devotion, and undying energy. Stability of character, industrious habits, physical energy, moral strength, mental force, and benevolent feelings are characteristics indispensible to a valuable communist. A Community of such members has an inexhaustible mine of wealth, though not in possession of one dollar."

The importance of Skaneateles is the importance of the character of the membership, and the observations of the founder, Mr. Collins, are words of wisdom, to be studied and pondered by all who seek to establish colonies or who expect to enter them. Self-examination should precede examination by the group, for the examination is certain to follow, whether intended or not.

THE BETHEL - AURORA COMMUNITIES
Bethel, 1844 to 1880 — Aurora, 1856 to 1911

Not important because of their achievements, but deserving of passing mention, were the Bethel and Aurora Communities. Bethel was established in 1844 in Shelby County, Missouri, and was made up in part by Rappites and some of those who had followed off the bogus Count de Leon. Dr. Wm. Kiel was its founder. Bethel lasted until 1880, so that in period of duration it showed success. The community owned 5,000 acres of good land and was prosperous. It provided the members, mostly Germans, with an abundance of good things to eat. At one time Bethel had 1000 members, but there were many secessions in the early days before success had attended their efforts, and at one single secession 250 members left. At the time of dissolution there were about 175 members. The Community was founded on a religious basis. Seceders could take with them whatever property they had brought in. They had a strange mixture of individualism and collectivism, but in the years of maturity the colony preserved harmony and happiness for its members. There was no constitution or by-laws. The Bethel band became famous for many miles.

The Aurora Community was founded in 1856 in Marion County, Oregon, by Dr. Kiel. Applicants for membership were at first paid wages and received on probation. There was no money consideration in the terms of membership. The land in both communities was for years held by Dr. Kiel, but eventually it was parceled out and title deeds were given. However, this made no difference in the Community life, showing how well grounded they were in their collectivism. At the time of dissolution there were 250 members at Aurora. There was no friction, and the dissolution was made easy by the fact that property had previously been deeded. The reason for dissolution was the death of Dr. Kiel. No one had been trained to take his place, and, though many were not in favor of the separation, it seemed to have been regarded as the only course to take. The properties were valued at nearly $200,000 when the change was made.

COLORADO CO-OPERATIVE COMMUNITY
1894 to 1910

This was what might be termed a temporary co-operative. It is strange how many people can recognize the benefits of co-operation, yet use them only so long as it may be necessary to reach a point where they may go back into competition and individualism.

The Colorado Co-operative Company was organized in 1894, and the site of its operations were Tabegauche Park in Montrose county, Colorado. The scenery was described as being beautiful; the elevation was 4800 to 5400 feet, with snow-capped mountains surrounding. The Company went through the usual troubles due to lack of adequate financing, with the consequent dissension; yet it held together and completed the chief work it set out to do—bring water to the land for irrigating.

Eugene Hopkins, a personal friend of the compiler of this volume, and a member of the Llano Co-operative Colony, writes from Healdsburg, California, as follows:

"I was a member and active worker for ten years in the Colorado Co-operative Company at Nucla, Colorado. I held positions on the board of directors and was ditch superintendent and water distributor for three seasons after the ditch was completed. Enclosed you will find some literature in regard to this co-operative ditch colony which was organized in 1894.

"The main object of this colony was to build an irrigation ditch. This canal was seventeen miles long from the headgate to the initial point on the parks, and was built thru a mountainous country which required not only ditches, but stretches of flume and also large trestles over canyons; one trestle was over 100 feet high. Much blasting of rock was required for flume beds. It cost over $100,000 and had a capacity of 60 feet of water. It was a big undertaking to be built by men without capital.

"This irrigation project was not declared completed until about the year 1910. The Colorado Co-operative Company built this ditch by co-operation, but when the ditch was completed, the members of the company went on to their land on which they had filed and proved up and started farming individually. Co-operation then ceased and no more enterprises were carried on in this manner."

The colony published "The Altrurian," a weekly newspaper, for several years. The issue of August 16, 1899, carries a long address by one of the members in which he reviewed some of the troubles through which they were going. They had attempted a task which was almost beyond them, and with their handicaps of lack of finance and equipment, they were making slow and difficult progress. Their diet was limited to the most frugal and plain fare, and they lacked sufficient feed for their animals—handicaps that have been common to co-operative colonies.

The by-laws of the company show that nine directors constituted a board, holding office for one year. Officers of the concern were bonded at $1,000 each. An election to remove the directors could be called by a petition signed by a majority of the stock holders. The plan was to employ stockholders of the association, though not all of the mwere guaranteed employment, and they were warned against coming without being given permission by the directors. It was also provided that the General Manager could deprive members of work for wilful negligence or refusal to perform reasonable service.

A statement sent out under date of June 25, 1902, showed assets of $121,985.92, with losses of $224 and gains of $681 for the period of five preceding months. These were evidently operated on a profit plan at the time; those reporting were the sawmill, blacksmith shop, freighting, dairy, boarding houses, store, ——— camp, and harness shop. The asset column of the statement listed a store, harness shop, blacksmith shop, printery, drug store, dairy, garden, sawmill, lumber and boxes, boarding houses, livestock consisting of 29 horses and mules and 15 cows and calves. The timber land was appraised at $500.

Among the provisions of the constitution and by-laws intended to protect the colony against individual enterprise and selfishness, was one which stipulated that the company should control all public utilities, and no franchise should be given to individuals. All members should be entitled to water rights at the pro-rated cost of the ditch. All credits for labor above the actual needs of the members were to be funded upon the company's books until the ditch was finished, when they should be payable in any product of the company or property.

But as stated in Mr. Hopkins' letter, the co-operative features were abandoned when the ditch was finished and water was turned on to the land. Nevertheless, here was a good example of a co-operative association, which, despite many problems and much inner turmoil, was able to keep steadily going from 1894 until 1910—surely a pretty good record under the circumstances which were faced.

CELESTA SECOND ADVENTISTS

"It would be interesting," comments Hinds, "to know how many communistic Societies have been based upon the doctrine of Christ's second advent. This was the foundation of Shakerism * * *. Eric Janson, founder of Bishop Hill Community, had a similar idea regarding himself. That, too, was the basic idea of the Harmonites * * * " Hinds mentions several others, among them being Celesta, founded by Peter Armstrong as a Second-Adventist Community. It prophesied the coming of Christ in 1843 or soon after. Armstrong was convinced that 144,000 persons were to be gathered together. This number also appears in the religious beliefs of other groups, the House of David among them. Armstrong thought it was his duty to begin gathering the select, and he secured a desolate location in the Allegheny mountains in Sullivan County, Pennsylvania, 2500 acres being the site. With his family he cleared 100 acres in 11 years, put up four houses, two barns, a sawmill and some smaller buildings. A neighbor commented that "it cost $40 an acre to clear the land, and it was worth $5 when cleared."

His religious zeal led Armstrong to deed the land to Almighty God, tho it was subsequently sold for taxes and purchased by a son of the founder of Celesta. Not more than 20 persons ever resided in the Community, but as their paper reached a circulation of 3000, Hinds concludes that many thousands might have gone into the barren wilderness with those whose misdirected zeal led them to found Celesta. Hinds included the account of Celesta as an example of what energy without wisdom might do and how it might work great misfortune to many persons. Celesta failed, however, before many were drawn into it, the fanaticism of its founder being sufficient to finally bring publicity which exposed the facts.

ADONAI - SHOMO

This community was founded at Athol, Massachusetts, in 1861, by about ten persons led by a Quaker, Frederick T. Howland, who became a Second Adventist. The community was chartered in 1876 under state laws. It lasted about 35 years. They became known as Fullerites because they settled in the property of Leonard Fuller. The leader, Howland, held to the theory of the immortal life, as did many of the religious sects, among them being the Swedes under Eric Janson, and the Koreshans under Dr. Teed. The death of Howland was a shock to his devout followers, just as was the death of Janson and Teed to their followers, who accepted their leaders' assertions literally. A man by the name of Cook became leader and instituted such revolting practices as led to his indictment by the grand jury and subsequent imprisonment.

However, the Community changed somewhat and prospered for some years, eventually owning 840 acres of land, a large unitary building, and an increased membership which reached about 30 at the most. It could not hold its younger members. The property was sold in 1897 for $4,390 to satisfy creditors. The buildings were quite large and well-built.

ST. NAZIAZ COLONY

This was a community of Roman Catholics, emigrants from Germany, who settled in Manitowoc County, Wisconsin. They settled in the wilderness, buying land at $3.50 an acre, purchasing 3840 acres. It was originally held by its founder, Father Oschwald, in trust, but on his death the society incorporated and took charge of the property after some legal difficulties. The members were celibate, each sex having its unitary buildings. The life was communal. A letter directed to the Society failed to bring a reply, but it may still be in existence.

THE BRUEDERHOFF COMMUNITIES

These were made up of Mennonites under Jacob Hutter, who go further than most of their brethren and do not engage in traffic for profit, nor take usury nor use tobacco. They have nothing to do with the usual forms of recreation, take no part in politics, and do not vote or hold office. They are Communists because they believe Christ was a communist. They came from Southern Russia, but are of German extraction.

The first of the Hutterites came in 1862 when the Hutterische colony was formed on the James river in South Dakota. Others followed, and several communities were founded. Efforts to get in touch with them to learn of development during the last 20 years were not successful, and it may be that they are no longer in existence. They had a total of more than 30,000 acres of land and several hundred members during the first years of the present century.

BROTHERHOOD OF THE NEW LIFE

Thomas Lake Harris founded a belief which took this name and which had adherents in several countries. Though born in England, he became very widely known as minister in a New York church and formed a Community in Virginia in 1851. They claimed they had the site of the ancient Garden of Eden. It was to have been a city of harmony and refuge; but, evidently, the original serpent was still in hiding, for quarrels soon broke out, and the members left in about two years.

Fourteen years later another community was established in New York state with a rather remarkable aggregation of colonists which included a number of children, sixty adults, five ministers, a number of Japanese, a man of literary fame, and a member of the English nobility. This was in 1869. They had about 2,000 acres of farm and vineyard lands, and one of the chief occupations was the manufacture of wines for medicinal purpose. They had storage for 65,000 gallons and were establishing industries when the colony collapsed. Later another effort was made in California, near Santa Rosa, but a woman who was permitted to live in the colony for a period published in the newspapers such accusations against Harris and his associates that the whole neighborhood arose and the colonists were forced to leave.

MME. MODJESKA'S COLONY

This was founded in Cracow, Poland, in 1876, by a group of distinguished people, most famous among whom was Mme. Helena Modjeska, who had become wearied of the stage. It numbered among its members also Henry Sienkiewiez, later to become widely known as the author of "Quo Vadis." There were artists and writers and musicians. In fact Hinds refers to it as a "Polish Brook Farm." This brilliant aggregation of talented people organized in Cracow, but came to Orange County, near Los Angeles, California, the following year, where they spent $54,000 in a short time as a community, besides the individual expenditures of the members. They knew little of the practical methods to employ, and while they greatly enjoyed the brief life of their colony, it was not a financial success, and finally had to disband. Not long ago this land was offered for sale at fabulous prices, and the fact that it was at one time colonized by Modjeska was made much of by the promoters. The social life of the colony was highly developed, as may well be imagined, but there was little practical work done, and it is to be feared that the Californians were none too scrupulous in their dealings with the European colonists.

SHALAM, OR THE CHILDREN'S COLONY

This was founded by Dr. J. B. Newbrough, who wrote a Bible which he called Oahspee, claiming that he wrote it on the typewriter while guided by unseen spirits. The colony was not a success. The purpose was to bring orphan and unfortunate children and create a great institution which would make useful citizens of them. Much of the funds were contributed by A. M. Howland, about 1,000 acres of land in the Masilla Valley of New Mexico being secured for the colony. It was founded in 1884, but by 1901 was being offered for sale. The loss was about $300,000. It perished for want of financial and moral support.

A COLONY IN PANAMA

From a copy of the Llano Colonist published in 1916, we take the following brief account of a colony attempted in Panama. Fred Mutchler visited the Llano Colony in California and gave a short talk on what had been attempted by him and others.

"Mr. Mutchler gave a brief synopsis of the co-operative colony in Panama, which was widely reported to have failed. Mr. Mutchler was its president and knew the real cause of failure. He said that it was impossible to receive or send out mail without its being censored. Money sent from the states would be returned to the sender; letters from members of the colony to outsiders were opened and all reference to the colony deleted; and all advertising matter rigidly excluded from the mails. The colony was under strict military rule, making co-operation impossible among the thirty-five members. After the colony disbanded transportation was "kindly" furnished to the members, and in some instances jobs given to some on the Canal zone. The real reason that the army did not want a colony started in Panama was because the zone is to be extended ten miles farther, which would include the colony lands, and the natural fear of Socialism."

THE LORD'S FARM
(About Twenty Years of Life)

There have been many colonies which have appeared utterly fantastic, but none of them are surpassed by "The Lord's Farm" in Bergen County, New Jersey. Yet it compels admiration; for, however impractical it may appear to have been from the account from which the facts herein given are taken, yet the sincerity and the earnestness and the remarkable fortitude and extraordinary non-resistant policy of "Paul" makes it worthy of space all out of proportion to its economic value. We are indebted to a reprint from The Open Court of October, 1919, entitled "Anarchism and the Lord's Farm" by Theodore Schroeder for the information used here.

"In the old life of sin-in-the-flesh he had another name. Now he lives in the spiritual rebirth. When the divinity within him came to rule his life, he was rechristened as Paul Blaudin Mnason. Some hailed him the New Christ, and others reviled him as the Anti-Christ. Scoffers called him 'the boss of the Angel Dancers.' When I told him that I was going to write about him under the title of 'Anarchism at the Lord's Farm,' he almost lost his spiritual poise in protest against being identified with anarchists. And yet he lived the life of Anarchism without professing or even knowing its doctrines. When the more conscious anarchists claimed him, he hated them probably because they professed the doctrine without the life. And yet for twenty years, he with others, worked out an experiment at living the life of the anarchist-communist * * *

"When this latter-day Paul first acknowledged the supreme authority of the 'divinity' within him * * * he went among those who advertised their liberality as well as those of conspicuous orthodoxy. Everywhere he met with more or less violent hostility. The 'liberals' denied him free speech because he was a 'nut.' The orthodox called the police or threw him out of their places of worship, because 'they could not bear the closer, purer light from this son of God.' * * * Later on by virtue of the 'divinity within him' the latter-day Paul cured a very sick maiden of 'an incurable disease.' Thru this miracle the way was opened, 'the Lord's Farm' was established, and there Christian liberty reigned supreme. At the Lord's Farm unconscious anarchists or conscious Christian communists, established a Utopia, a miniature edition of heaven upon earth. Here many of the despised of the world found spiritual and economic regeneration.

"In the kingdom of Heaven there could be no private property, nor any privileges but the privilege of service. Paul refused a deed to the Lord's Farm because it implied too much ownership. Even a mere formal lease from sister Blaudina was a bad compromise between the godly ideal and the human way of doing things. A lease was taken, however, but that did not give any one within the sacred precincts greater liberty or authority than was enjoyed by any of the rest. Blaudina was not the name her parents gave her. By this new name she symbolized the fact that she had been physically and spiritually reborn. The godless called her the 'beautiful little angel dancer of the Lord's Farm.' No books of account were kept at the Lord's Farm. In the kingdom of God no record of material things could be preserved. * * *

"To combine practice with profession is a constant reproach to those who only pretend, and these are always resentful. So friction arose between the Lord's Farmers and their materially-minded, spiritually-pretentious neighbors. Reviling was followed by persecution. * * * Mobs cut Paul's hair and pulled his whiskers. This was followed by arrests for Sabbath breaking and blasphemy; conspiracy to defraud, and running a disorderly house; kidnapping and raping and almost everything else in the criminal code. Convictions were actually secured against Paul for the blasphemy of allowing himself to be adored as a Son of God. * * * The Lord's Farmers thought that if God's law is to prevail, human laws must be ignored and lawyers should not be employed in the defense of God's own. Turn the other cheek, was the rule. * * * In some of these persecutions the indictments called Paul by the name of Mason T. Huntsman. Most strenuously he repudiated this name. In fact, he was just as anxious to disown the name as were his relatives and namesakes to have him do so. Some of these reside on Fifth Avenue, facing Central Park in New York City.

"Free newspaper advertising followed in abundance upon prosecution. Publicity brought all those whom the world calls 'cranks,' all those who have theories of superiority with which to explain their status as the world's misfits. The Jew, the Chinaman, the Christian Scientist, and the Papist, the Methodist and the New Thoughter, the Swami, and the Christian clergyman, spiritualists, theosophists, atheists, anarchists, and socialists—all these came and prayed or cursed, worshiped, or persecuted, soothed or quarreled, according to various understanding and temperament. They came and went as they pleased. Some stayed for hours, some for days, and a few for years. During 18 years the Lord's Farm fed three thousand persons. Some were cleansed in body and some in soul. Many were restored to self-respect and social usefulness. All this was done without asking any questions or imposing any conditions * *. From each according to his ability, to each according to his needs * * *."

But this brought some strange characters, and not all of them came for the good of the community, according to Mr. Schroeder's lively account. He mentions one Daniel Haines, who he believes was slightly demented. Daniel claimed he had the Holy Ghost in large quantity and that it challenged the righteousness of Paul. He took the hinges off the doors so that the people outside might hear the disputes within. He tried to discredit Paul and his faithful band, and shouted aloud his intent. On one occasion Daniel grappled with Paul, but the sturdy Paul put the obstreperous one down, then released him and asked "What next?" Failing in his physical force, Daniel broke all of the dishes, suffering no rebuke and no objections; the others merely looked on. At this thrilling juncture the police came and arrested all of those at Lord's Farm, though the reason had nothing to do with the startling proceedings which confronted their astonished eyes. The charge was conspiracy to defraud the owners of the farm. Dishes were taken as evidence, however, of a disorderly house. Nothing came of the charge, tho they remained in jail for six months. They were, however, convicted on a charge of conducting a disorderly house because of the breaking of the dishes. Paul and Phoebe were sentenced to state's prison, but Daniel was released. Later all were reunited and all forgiven. Then Daniel took a horse and wagon, saying that as all things were free at Lord's Farm, he chose the horse and wagon. No opposition was interposed, but a few days later a farmer returned the horse and wagon, having found them abandoned on the road.

Charles Hammond, infidel, was drawn out of curiosity, and tho he did not espouse the religion of the Lord's Farmers, he stayed for many months and was one of their best workers, adopting their manner of living. At the same time, came one Louis, fanatically religious, with a call to preach, but no call to work. Charles the non-religious, objected strenuously to having to support Louis the religious. He reported to Paul, but the latter would do nothing. Charles struck Paul, but the latter merely asked: "Have you finished, Charles? If not, don't stop." But Charles was ashamed and did nothing more in abusing Paul, returning to work after being thus quietly rebuked.

Many hoboes came, and the neighbors complained, probably with good cause, that the Lord's Farm was a magnet which drew more hoboes into the neighborhood than they were entitled to. All were made welcome without question or examination, physical or otherwise. One of them was so pleased with this that he stayed, and asked that his breakfast be served in the afternoon, as he did not like to get up early. One day Paul took the man's breakfast to his room, explaining that they did not want to put him to the inconvenience of having to go downstairs, and assuring him they wished him to be happy. But this cured the hobo, who never again remained in bed after the usual breakfast time, and who became a fair worker. Paul's method of getting the lazy to work was to assure them that they should not work so long as they could be happy in idleness.

A fanatically religious woman with some Eve-like ideas came and began pursuing Paul, whom she said was Adam. But Paul evaded the woman, who insisted in running true to Eden costumes as well as customs and reduced her clothing at times to about fig-leaf proportions, or less. Paul avoided any embarrassing relations with the woman, and finally a certain angelic Granville with Adam-like notions appeared. The neighbors were appalled at the actions of the couple and said that their spiritual freedom went far in excess of what was usually understood to be spiritual and partook very strongly of what might be understood by the ungodly as sexual license. However, Granville soon decided to establish a kingdom in Philadelphia and finally went to that populous center.

A certain Willson from England tried to supplant Paul, and gave him terrible tongue-lashings, to which the unperturbed Paul replied: "That's fine. Now can't you tell me something new about myself?" And finally Willson withdrew, defeated by the submissive non-resistance of Paul.

"The free publicity given to the communistic aspect of the Lord's Farm," continues Schroeder, "served as a lure for irreligious socialists and anarchist doctrinaires. These came with their rule of thumb to prove to Paul that he was not consistent with Marx, Mme. Bakunin, or Tucker, or someone else. Paul knew nothing of these strange unscriptural doctrines and he cared less. He was concerned only with living the divine life. He would tell these critics that they were only intellectual garbage cans peddling the dead and decaying material of other minds; fooling themselves by thinking that this rotten doctrine-stuff could upset the ways and work of God, or that God could or would descend to the ways of men. Others he would advise to hang crape on their noses in memory of their dead brains."

Alice Page came for treatment—mental, spiritual, and physical. But at about the same time, five holy rollers also came, and they kept the place in such pandemonium that Alice could not rest. Neither could the neighbors, who loudly voiced their complaints; Paul was probably also growing impatient with the antics of the invaders. One of these exasperated neighbors, a lawyer, protested. Paul told him the people on "Lord's Farm" had all rights and freedom, and he would do nothing. He added, however: "Here all are free; you may do as you please, even as they are free." The astute lawyer took this as a hint and acted as his new-found freedom permitted, which was to accelerate the leaving of the shouters by using the toe of his shoe in an energetic and vigorous manner. Paul did not interfere.

But Paul was not proof against all exasperations. One of the Lord's Farmers had an adopted son, and used the stick to coerce the little fellow to work. Paul stood it as long as he could, till finally his temper broke the leash which had held it so long and he used a club on the man who had whipped the boy. Unfortunately for the Lord's Farm, this man was owner of the land, and he at once started proceedings to oust Paul, succeeding in a short time.

The value of the Lord's Farm experiment may not be great, and it is somewhat in line with the experiment made by Gerald Geraldson in his Army of Industry at Auburn, California. Yet they show the tenacity of life possible under conditions which seem to most people to contain the seeds of dissolution in their very inception. The strange thing is that they exist so long, when colonies much better prepared, apparently, to face the world's problems as they contact colonies, do not exhibit anything like the same ability for solidity and life. Schroeder comments, "* * * they were excessively exploited and martyrized without making any lasting contribution to the triumph of their dominant desires, that is, of democracy, or liberty, or of their concept of religion." And he concludes that "their desires were too far ahead of their time * * * and their understanding of human behavior was very inadequate."

NEVADA COLONY
1916—1918

One of the most extensively advertised community colonization projects of the last two decades was the Nevada Colony, located at Fallon, Nevada. It was established in May, 1916, by C. V. Eggleston and others, and finished its career in a tragic manner in the summer of 1918.

Eggleston had acted as fiscal agent for the Llano Co-operative Colony of Llano, California, in 1915 and part of 1916. He brought to the Llano enterprise the methods of the stock promoter; and, though he came with a reputation as a life-long Socialist, his manner of selling memberships was not satisfactory to the Llano colonists, and early in 1916 his connection was severed. Eggleston had meanwhile gained a somewhat meager knowledge of community life, and a quite complete list of names of prospective members. Thus equipped, he instituted the Nevada Colony. For a time this was linked with the Llano Colony, but the separation was made early in 1916.

Eggleston was successful in securing the right to use the names of men prominent in the Socialist movement, and he traded on their names vigorously. Some of these claimed that he used their names without authority, and there is reason to believe that they are correct in this statement. Fred D. Warren and "Baldy" Richardson lent their names willingly, but many others were used. Thousands of persons had much faith in these prominent Socialists, and a great spurt was thus given to the securing of memberships and the accompanying cash which floated the enterprise and financed it.

The Llano Colony repudiated its connection with the Nevada Colony in every way it could and was at considerable expense to make this clear. That Eggleston had been for a number of months connected with the former, and because the headquarters of the Llano Colony were in Reno, much confusion resulted.

The location was a good one. The Lahonton dam impounded a vast quantity of water for irrigation and the lands were well irrigated. A good variety of crops could be grown. The weakness of the situation was that the lands of the colony were not contiguous, and that they were not owned by the colony. There was loss of time and effort and interest because of these facts. However, there was probably sufficient grounds for believing in the success of the venture had there not been other and more serious causes for failure.

One of the most dangerous of these was the bargain-counter membership rates. A campaign was put on to sell memberships and permit residence on the payment of $250. To spur prospective members to action, a time limit was placed on the low-priced offer. The result was to bring in a quick flow of cash, but the quality of members was not given attention. What resulted was an influx of persons, many of whom had but vague and indefinite ideas of the conditions of colony life. They, in many cases, were influenced chiefly by the hope of bettering their material conditions, and gave considerably less thought to the principles underlying co-operative communities.

The plan of the organization was that of a stock corporation. It was modeled in most respects after the Llano Colony, and some who had been in Llano went to the Nevada colony, tho not many.

Trouble reached an acute stage in December, when a circular was issued under the title "Nevada Colony Corporation a Fake," J. H. Barkley and others subscribing sworn statements. Some of these were members, some ex-members. It accused Eggleston of being a Czar, of summarily cancelling contracts of W. G. Barker and family and others, and advising that the colony did not have the enterprises and institutions which its literature and its organ, "The Nevada Colonist," advertised. The statement stipulated in detail that the Nevada Colony had "no hotel, no mattress factory, no ink factory, no grocery or dry goods store, no cabinet factory, no movie picture show, no blueing factory, no tannery * * *. Their only means of living is the money coming in from new members joining the colony." The circular also charged C. V. Eggleston with getting $250 from each $1000 paid in, that the colony had one motor truck, mortgaged for $1400, instead of the seven advertised. The sworn portion of the circular claimed that all the property of the colony was mortgaged to its full value.

In the March issue of "The Nevada Colonist," Eggleston replied to the circular, saying that those responsible for the circular performed little or no useful labor, but spent their time trying to disrupt the colony, resulting in their being discharged. Eggleston made the statement that one of the malcontents had traded property for his stock, but refused to trade back except on conditions causing a loss to the man with whom he had traded. Eggleston claimed that the equipment for the factories and institutions referred to in the circular were purchased and were stored ready to be operated. Eggleston also made the statement in his defense that the colony shipped in June, 1916, a carload of hogs, that in January of 1917 a car of hogs and cattle; that the previous November 800 pounds of turkeys at 28 cents a pound had been sold, that in about 9 months $1500 worth of cream had been marketed, and that the production of alfalfa at market prices amounted to $15,000.

In the same issue of the paper was a report of a stockholders' investigation committee which showed that the colony had title to 1640 acres of land.

The Nevada Colonist also claimed that 95 per cent of all who came and investigated became members if they were financially able to do so.

A visitor writing in the same paper under date of January 17, 1917, reported that he found thirty men and fifty women and children, 1600 acres of land, with 400 of it in alfalfa, 73 milch cows, both Jerseys and Holsteins in the herd, 70 horses, two registered bulls and two registered stallions included; 800 thoroughbred white leghorn hens and 40 hen turkeys. The man who wrote it was R. E. Bray, later to become very prominent in the affairs of the colony.

In answer to questions submitted to him, E. C. Bennett, later a member of the Llano Co-operative Colony in Louisiana, wrote:

"Eggleston was painted by R. E. Bray, who was as bad, as being the greatest thief of all time. He got big commissions for selling stock and made money from the project. When the crash came, the colony had about 30 beautiful adobe houses and had done some leveling on the land.

"There was no social life while I was there (Sept. 16, 1917 to March 11, 1918) except the weekly meeting, usually Sunday, for debating and voting. There were no educational facilities. Neighbors viewed the colony with suspicion and hostility, some withdrawing what they had put into it. I was much impressed by the false notion held by many that they came in to live better than they had outside, and finally the hatred which was manifested. The colonists acted exceedingly comradely toward each other at first. Then came the quarrel which became more bitter up to the time I left. When it became known outside that the colony was divided over government, money stopped coming. As nothing was being sold, necessaries could no longer be bought; hence, the end. There were no industries, and all income was derived from the sale of memberships and from loans. The activities consisted of growing wheat, white potatoes, garden truck, alfalfa, etc., and in making adobe brick and in putting up buildings. There were about 125 persons when I went there, and 150 when I left. I think this is the greatest population ever attained.

"I think success would have been possible if the colony had owned the land. But the lack of ownership, the debts, and the want of natural resources combined to make failure probable. The immediate causes were the big families, rather high standard of living, and the final split into factions. The quarrel arose immediately after the director's meeting in October, 1917. R. E. Bray held proxies so that he elected the whole board. The quarrel which followed became one between 'intellectuals' and 'laborers.' Bray claims the credit of having expelled Eggleston from the colony, but he seems to have had but little better idea than Eggleston as to the fundamentals necessary to community success."

In 1918 members began taking up mineral lands, and many of them left the colony for this purpose, though they may not have severed their connection. The war took some of the men, and intensified the problems that confronted the group. No money was coming. The failure which had been imminent for many months and freely prophesied, followed in the summer of 1918, one woman committing suicide in her discouragement. Bennett says that bloodshed was narrowly averted on a number of occasions when passions were inflamed. Another authority tells of a draftee resisting officers, hiding in the hills, being furnished food, presumably by the colonists, and killing the officer who came to arrest him. This resulted in high feeling against the colonists, many of whom were probably entirely ignorant of the entire affair.

The Nevada Colony can be analyzed as an abortive effort to establish a Community without sufficient funds, without a good foundation, and by persons with only the most meager knowledge of the technique required. Eggleston used the intensive methods of modern business and was accused repeatedly, both in Llano and in the Nevada colonies, of being unscrupulous in his methods of securing money. However this may be, he had little conception of the real problems, and those he attracted were materialists, attracted chiefly because they expected to better themselves. They were impatient, quarrelsome, fault-finding, and very lacking in the ideals necessary to the enterprise in which they had enlisted. Notwithstanding a quite definite understanding of the Marxian philosophy and the theory of economic determinism, they had very little of the real understanding of the humanitarism necessary to success where all residents constitute a family. Their failure was foreshadowed by this lack of real idealism; no mere material successes could have made up for its lack, and the hardships due to lack of incoming funds merely hastened what would have probably come about sooner or later anyway.

It is apparent to many that the Nevada Colony was to its originator, C. V. Eggleston, merely a business enterprise and he brought to bear on it all of his training as a salesman and a business man. But this attempt to commercialize the ideals and hopes of humanity, this attempt to establish a Com-

74

munity of persons unskilled in the ways of business and opposed on principle to commercialism, putting their structure on a foundation of intense
commercialism, was trying to do the impossible.

Many of those who went into the Nevada Colony were idealists, but
many were bargain seekers, and their purposes were not based on idealism
but on their own hopes and ambitions and selfish desires; they brought in
with them traits which defeated their own hopes and purposes.

Communities
of the Present

THE SHAKER COMMUNITIES
1776 to Present Time

Some members of the Society of Quakers formed themselves into a group of which Jane and James Wardley were leaders, holding meetings of a spiritualistic nature. This was in 1747. The members were often seized in their meetings with a mighty trembling; at other times they sang their songs of praise, shouting and leaping for joy; sometimes they would be compelled to shake their limbs or run or walk, "with a variety of other operations or signs, swiftly passing and repassing each other." Because of these strange exercises they were called Shakers. They were persecuted, and this brought them new members. Ann Lee joined them, and in 1770 professed, while in prison, to having had a great revelation of Christ's Kingdom.

In 1776 Mother Ann, as Ann Lee came to be called, started a settlement at Niskayuna, New York, seven miles from Albany. Their fame spread, and soon many joined them. Persecution again followed and many were imprisoned.

The rules governing the admission of members into Shaker Societies were:

1—All persons uniting with the Shaker Society, in any degree, must do it freely and voluntarily, according to their own faith and unbiased judgment.

2—In the testimony of the Society, both public and private, no flattery or any undue influence is used.

3—No considerations of property are ever made use of by this Society to induce any person to join it, nor to prevent any person from leaving it.

4—Any person becoming a member must rectify all his wrongs and as fast and as far as possible discharge all just and legal claims.

5—It is an established principle in the Society that children who are faithful and obedient to their parents until they became of age are justly entitled to their equal portion of the estate of their parents, whether they continue with the Society or not.

The government was simple. There were several Ministeries, each consisting when fully organized of two brethren and two sisters, and each having special supervision of two or most Societies. Subordinate to the Ministries there are in every fully organized community, or family in each society, two elders and two elderesses, having special charge of its spiritual affairs, and two Deacons and two Deaconesses having charge of temporal affairs, these latter being subordinate to the Elders and Elderesses as they are in turn to the Ministry. The Deacons may be specially appointed as acting trustees to hold titles to the property of the family to which they belong and to manage its businesses.

In Shaker communities the women have equal rank with the men, frequently holding superior offices and managing their own departments fully.

A requirement of Shaker communities is that all must labor a certain number of hours daily and must subordinate their own wishes respecting choice of industries to the general interest of the Society as expressed thru its officers. Early Shakers lived rigid lives from which all beauty was eliminated, but in later years music and flowers were not only permitted but to some degree encouraged, and the austerity of their lives has been greatly modified. Pictures of individual members were prohibited because of the tendency to idolatry, the liability of causing personal vanity, and the consequent disunity which might result from preference given to individuals thus noticed.

In the matter of diet, many of the Societies of the Shakers were quite advanced, and, as a result of this progress, together with hygienic wisdom, sickness was almost entirely eliminated from among them. Pork was not used for food, and many used no meat whatever. Liquors were never used.

The Shakers have had to depend for their new members largely upon the unfortunates who flock to them for homes when they find the struggle for existence too hard, and upon orphans and the children of poor people. Despite what might seem to have been poor material with which to work, the Shakers have developed able thinkers, writers, speakers, and men of marked business capacity. They are credited with a long list of useful inventions, among them being a mower and reaper, a circular saw, a printing press, a planing machine, a tongue-and groove machine, a revolving harrow, a pea-sheller, cut nails, metallic pen, etc.

The form of government was theocratic rather than democratic, and Mr. Hinds, in commenting on it, asks the question whether it is not "wisest to so conduct affairs that every one shall feel, not only that he is personally interested in the general prosperity, but that he contributes to it according to the measure of his ability."

The Shakers were celibates and had a total of fifteen societies with a membership at one time of 5000 persons, with twenty-one different Shaker communities, the largest being Mount Lebanon, New York. They owned large farms and a very large acreage of land, which they have been selling of late years. Their membership is now quite small..

"The Shakers themselves are persuaded," says Mr. Hinds in "American Communities," "that the celibate condition is superior to any other, and raises them above the worldly or generative place. That every human passion may be exercised in the spirit of purity they have not yet learned, and we must respect their earnest efforts to separate themselves from every fleshly temptation that they may lead sinless lives. They do not wholly condemn marriage, as many suppose; but, on the contrary, they admit that it is a natural and proper relation for those who have not been called to the higher or resurrection order."

They welcomed scientific propagation of the human race, and James S. Prescott is quoted as saying: "What is the reason man does not know how to improve the race as well as he knows how to improve the ox, the sheep, the horse, and the feathered tribes? He does know how; it is by observing the same law, working by the same rule, and minding the same things. * * * As things are, multitudes of persons of both sexes are no more suitable to reproduce human beings in the image of God than the roach-backed, crooked-legged, spindle-shanked, slab-sided Indian ponies are suitable for generating the best types of the noble horse."

Of the many thousands of children placed in the Societies for one cause and another, very few remained after reaching years of maturity, or developed other than ignoble traits of character. One member is quoted as saying: "Since I came here forty-nine years ago, we have taken in young people enough to make a continuous line half a mile long, and I alone remain." Another said: "Out of eighty boys that went to school in the course of five winters, not one beside myself remained till he was 20 years old."

The hygienic conditions of living, perhaps more than celibacy, contributed to the long life of the Shakers. A list of aged persons from two societies shows remarkably long lives. Hinds gives it as follows:

12 members died at 90	3 members died at 97
12 members died at 92	1 member died at 98
8 members died at 91	1 member died at 99
5 members died at 93	1 member died at 100
3 members died at 94	1 member died at 102
2 members died at 95	1 member died at 108
2 members died at 96	1 member died at 120

The Shakers were not free from lawsuits, but the same decision that was given in other cases of similar societies was rendered, and the society showed that its rights were superior to those of individual members, and its position was sustained in the courts.

Recently the Shakers have sold much of their holdings, and their numbers are much diminished. None of them are youthful. Modern youth is not attracted to this system of living, and celibacy does not prove alluring. There may be other reasons, but the facts remain that while the communism, the co-operative living of the Shakers, has been immensely successful, and while they have amassed wealth which has been estimated to run into ten or twelve million dollars, they have not been able to maintain their numbers and spread their beliefs. Their communities have existed since the time of the Revolutionary war, surely a record of achievement well worth considering.

When George T. Pickett visited the Shakers early in 1924, he reported to the writer that he found them wealthy, but with little hope of the perpetuation of the society, because many were well along in years and few new members were joining. One of their largest properties, in New Hampshire, was untenanted. Lack of interest has unquestionably been due largely to the preference for celibacy which has been followed.

A friend sends a clipping from a daily paper published in Ohio in September, 1922, from which we take the following:

There will be sold at public auction next week at South Union, Kentucky, the lands of the Shaker Community that was founded there in the middle of the last century. Not many years ago the Shaker Community in the vicinity of Cleveland sold its lands and the members scattered among other communities of the faith. * * *

The abandonment of the Kentucky colony is thought to mark the beginning of the end of Shakerism. It is estimated that there are living only about 200 aged men and women, followers of Ann Lee, who made one of the most successful experiments ever know in the history of the United States. The survivors of Shakerism will be gathered in a single community at New Lebanon, New York. * * *

Every Shaker community was a great financial success, and to-day the survivors have many thousands of dollars to keep them in comfort as long as they live and to leave as a memorial to their thrift * * * Celibacy was a cardinal doctrine of Shakerism, but their numbers were recruited by converts so that for several generations the sect was growing and progressive.

The passing of Shakerism as a religious and socialistic sect is not due to internal dissension or financial reverses. The spirit of the times has changed gradually, and in the past 25 years no effort has been made to recruit members. So the membership has slowly decreased. No one was ever detained by force in a Shaker community. If any member wished to depart at any time and go back into the world, he was given a liberal competence, sufficient to make him independent for life, and he left with the good will of his associates.

Efforts on the part of the author to get information from the headquarters at New Lebanon were not successful, probably as the Shakers have never sought publicity and did not care to encourage it.

THE AMANA COMMUNITY

Organized 1714 in Europe; Established in U. S. in 1842; Still in Existence

Two hundred and ten years have passed over the Amana Society, though its New World colonization dates back only to 1842. Yet with this respectable age of more than 80 years of continuous growth and progress, and with a prosperity that totals more than $2,000,000 when measured in dollars for its 1500 inhabitants, the society has made a good material showing and retains a vigor and vitality that insures it many more years. Its per capita wealth of $1333 is a respectable showing, perhaps more than many communities are able to show.

We are indebted for this account of the Amana Society chiefly to The Palimpsest, published monthly at Iowa City by the State Historical Society of Iowa, and much of the material is taken from the July, 1921, issue of that little magazine. Some additional matter is taken from the Brief History of the Amana Society, revised and issued in 1918.

In deference to the retiring disposition shown by the citizens of Amana, it is well to start this account with a paragraph of a letter received by the compiler of this volume from the Amana Society, a brief initialed note from which we excerpt the following: "It has always been our policy to avoid publicity and everything that appeared as propaganda; but whenever anything has to be published, we prefer to furnish correct information rather than to see many absurd statements published." And the information which is given in the following pages has the approval of the Amana Society and is in response to request for something authentic.

Says The Palimpsest:

"In one of the garden spots of Iowa there is a charming little valley through which the historic Iowa River flows peacefully to the eastward. A closer view reveals seven old-fashioned villages nestling among the trees or sleeping on the hillsides. About these seven villages stretch twenty-six thousand goodly acres clothed with fields of corn, pastures, meadows, gardens, orchards and vineyards, and seas of waving grain. Beyond and above, surrounding the little valley, are richly timbered hills forming as though by design a frame for this quaint picture of Amana — the home of the Community of True Inspiration.

"And what is Amana? To the traveller, viewing the fleeting landscape from the observation car of the Rocky Mountain Limited, it is a singular cluster of unpainted houses and barns amid battalions of vine-covered bean poles and blossoming onion tops, surrounded by well-tilled fields. To the speeding motorist on the River to River Road, bent on making the distance between Davenport and Des Moines in a day, it furnishes a curiously delightful stopping place for rest and refreshment and a fresh supply of gasoline.

80

"To the villagers themselves, with their aversion to mixing "philosophy and human science with divine wisdom," Amana with its villages and gardens, its orchards and vineyards, its mills and factories, its rich harvest fields and wooded hills, and its abiding peace and cheerfulness is the visible expression of the Lord's will: to them the establishment of villages, the growth and development of industries, and the success of communism are all incidental to the life and thought of the Community whose chief concern is spiritual. Born of religious enthusiasm and disciplined by persecution, it has ever remained primarily a Church. And so the real Amana is Amana the Church — Amana, the Community of True Inspiration.

"In language, in manners, in dress, in traditions, as well as in religious and economic institutions, the Community of True Inspiration is foreign to its surroundings — so much so that the visitor is at once impressed with the fact that here is something different from the surrounding world. In the eighteenth century the Inspirationists paid the penalty in the Old World for their non-conformity to established customs by imprisonment and exile: in the twentieth century they are objects of curiosity to their neighbors and the subject of no little speculation. The Inspirationist is by nature and by discipline given to attending quietly to his own business; and much impertinent inquiry on the part of visitors has intensified his reticence. But Amana has no secrets to hide from the world.

"It is apparent, however that that isolation from the "world" for which the Community of True Inspiration has so earnestly striven and which it has so jealously guarded for six generations becomes less and less easy to preserve. The railroad and airplane, the telephone and telegraph, the newspaper and magazine, the endless procession of automobiles, and the great World War have at last brought the Community and the "world" so close together that marked changes are taking place in the customs of the people and in their attitude toward life.

"To the German Mystics and Pietists of the sixteenth and seventeenth centuries the Community of True Inspiration traces its origin — developing into a distinct religious sect about the year 1714. Protesting against the dogmatism of the Lutheran Church and refusal to conform to its ritual, the Inspirationists were persecuted and prosecuted. They were fined, pilloried, flogged, imprisoned, legislated against, exiled, and stripped of their possessions.

"It was a simple faith — a belief in guidance through divine revelation —that held together the early congregations of Inspirationists despite humiliation and torture. * * * It was this simple faith that sustained the Community through years of persecution and trial in the Old World and through years of suffering and sacrifice in the New World.

"It is to the religious zeal and practical genius of Christian Metz, a young carpenter of Ronneburg, that the Community owes its greatest debt.

Even to this day the spell of the influence of this remarkable leader is felt throughout Amana.

"It was Christian Metz who first conceived the idea of leasing estates in common as a refuge for the faithful; and while the original intention had been to live together as a church, Metz foresaw that a system of communism would be the natural outcome of the mode of life which these people had been forced to adopt. And he foresaw that exorbitant rents and unfriendly governments in the Old World would one day make it necessary for the Inspirationists to find a home in the New World, 'where they and their children could live in peace and liberty.'

"It was in 1842 that a committee of four led by Christian Metz purchased the Seneca Indian Reservation — a tract of five thousand acres near Buffalo, Erie County, N. Y. Within four months of the purchase of the Reservation the first village of the Community was laid out and peopled. Five others were soon established, and more than eight hundred members crossed the water to join the group of pioneers."

A number of people also joined the Society from Canada, and as they owned some land there, the Society decided to locate two additional villages on it. One was at Caneborough, later changed to Kenneberg by the Society, about 45 miles northwest of Buffalo, and one near the Niagara River, 12 miles north of Buffalo, called Canada Ebenezer.

"Each village had its store, its school, and its church; soon there arose the cheerful hum of saw mills, woolen mills, and flour mills. A temporary constitution providing for 'common possession' was adopted, and the Community was formally organized under the name of 'Ebenezer Society.' For twelve years they toiled in the mills and factories and tilled the newly-broken fields when it became apparent that more land than was available so near the growing city of Buffalo would be necessary to accommodate the increasing membership. And once more a committee of four, with Christian Metz as its leader, was 'ordained and directed' to go forth to 'find a new home in the far West.' * * * Lands in Iowa County were described in such glowing terms that a purchase of nearly eighteen thousand acres was made by them without further delay. A better location or more valuable tract of land than the new site in Iowa could hardly be imagined. Through it ran the beautiful Iowa River bordered with the wonderful black soil of its wide valley. On one side were the bluffs and the uplands covered with a luxuriant growth of timber — promising an almost limitless supply of fuel and building material. There were a few quarries of sandstone and limestone along the river; while the clay in the hills was unexcelled for the manufacture of brick. On the other side of the river stretched the rolling prairie land.

"With a will they set to work to cut the timber and quarry the stone and build anew houses, shops, mills, factories, churches, and schoolhouses. They planted orchards and vineyards, and purchased flocks and herds.

They revived the old industries and started new ones.

"There was no rush to the country so gloriously described by the Iowa fore-guards — though no one can doubt the eagerness with which every member looked forward to the upbuilding of the new home. The removal from Ebenezer extended over a period of ten years and was carried thru with that prudence, judgment, and common sense which has always characterized these people in the conduct of their business affairs.

"While one detail of members prepared the new home in Iowa, the other looked to the profitable selling of the old estate in New York. As they found purchasers for the latter, they sent families to the former. To their business credit it is recorded that they were able to dispose of the whole of the eight thousand acre tract in the state of New York with all the improvements without the loss of a single dollar, notwithstanding such a sale presented great difficulties — for the six communistic villages and their peculiar arrangement of buildings, with mills, factories, and workshops had peculiarities which detracted from their value for individual uses.

"The first village on the Iowa purchase was laid out during the summer of 1855 on a sloping hillside north of the Iowa River, and it was called 'Amana' by Christian Metz — the word signifying 'remain true' or 'believe faithfully.' * * * Five more villages were laid out within a radius of six miles from Amana and were named in accordance with their locations, West Amana, South Amana, High Amana, East Amana, and Middle Amana. Modeled after the country villages of middle Europe, the houses of the 'Amana Colonies,' as they are commonly called, were clustered together on one long straggling street with several irregular offshoots, with the barns and sheds at one end, the factories and workshops at the other, and on either side the orchards, the vineyards, and the gardens.

"In the system of village life, which has been the great conservator of the Community's purity and simplicity, the Inspirationists have shown their farsightedness. The villages are near enough to one another to facilitate superintendence and to preserve a feeling of unity. At the same time they are far enough apart to maintain a simplicity of living, which would probably be impossible with the same number of people congregated in one place. By this means the Community, while taking advantage of every progressive step in the methods of agriculture and the processes of manufacture, has been able to sustain in its social, political, and religious life an insular position.

"Two steps of great importance were taken by the Community soon after its removal to Iowa. One was its incorporation under the laws of the State as the 'Amana Society' ; and the other was the adoption of a new constitution.

"The fundamental law of the Amana Society * * * provides simply and briefly a civil organization for a religious society. It is worthy of comment that the Amana Society still lives under the provisions of the instrument that has received the signature of every member of the Society since its adoption in December, 1859.

"The membership, numbering eight hundred when the Community migrated to New York and twelve hundred when the removal to Iowa took place, has increased to fifteen hundred at the present day. Bountiful harvests have rewarded their untiring industry; the products of their mills and factories have found a market from Maine to California; and in the books of the Auditors of Iowa and Johnson counties, their real and personal property was listed in 1920 at $2,102,984."

The official "Brief History of the Amana Society or Community of True Inspiration," revised in 1918, has this to say of the material phases of the colony:

"The increase in membership has been slow but steady up to a few years ago; for several years it remained stationary between 1700 and 1800, and now is about 1500. The Society operates two woolen mills, one at Amana and the other at Middle Amana. The power for these manufactories is furnished by the Iowa River through a canal 7 miles in length and by steam power plants. Besides these there is a flouring mill at Amana and one at West Amana, also 7 stores distributed through the various towns. These stores supply the wants of the members, as well as of the surrounding farming population. The Society raises nearly all the agricultural products required for its own use, several hundred hired laborers being employed for the heavier work. Nearly all the towns are provided with a water system fed from the canal or by deep wells. Each member is provided with board and dwelling, as provided for in the constitution. The meals are taken in large kitchen houses, where 30 to 50 people eat together, thus making cooking by individual families unnecessary. Children attend school throughout the year from the age of 5 to 14. The schools, part of the public school system, are graded and are conducted by teachers who are members of the Society. Religious meetings are held in large meeting houses, twice on Sunday and sometimes on week days, and a short prayer-meeting is held every evening. The services are presided over by one of the elders, of whom there are about 80 in all. No one at the present time has the gift of inspiration, as Christian Metz died in 1867, and Barbara Landmann in 1883, but the testimonies and writings left by these are read in all meetings.

"New members are not admitted except they first give proof of being fully in accord with the religious doctrine of the Society, and then they usually have to go through a period of probation. The trustees have the power to expel any member whose conduct is not according to the rules of the Society."

Continuing, the Palimpsest article says:

"And the difficulties of administration of so human an institution are apparent. Six generations of precept and practice in self-denial and brother-

ly love have not, of course, completely annihilated the dissatisfied and trouble-
some. Nor was there ever a congregation of fifteen hundred souls without
its hampering Brothers — those upon whom the responsibility of protecting the
highly cherished good name of the organization rests but lightly, those who
enjoy its material blessings and benefits, but are reluctant to share the burdens and cares and the necessary sacrifice.

"Under the terms of the constitution of the Amana Society such pre-
sumptuous members can be expelled as from any other church organization.
But such an expulsion, however, presents baffling complications since it in-
volves the actual turning out of house and home of the disturbing elements. It
is in the successful solution of such problems quite as much as in the business foresight of its administrative officers that one discovers the explanation
of the Community's long life. The predominating spirit is still the spirit of
the forefathers. Were it not so the Community could not be held together,
for the Amana Society is, after all, simply a voluntary association depending
for its perpetuity upon the general good will and good faith of its members.

"The Trustees elect annually on the second Tuesday of the month of
December out of their own number a President, a Vice-President, and a
Secretary. The incumbents are usually re-elected; for rotation in office has
never been a part of the Amana theory of government.

"In the month of June in each year the Trustees exhibit to the voting
members of the Society (who comprise, according to the by-laws, all male
members who have signed the constitution, all widows, and such female
members as are thirty years of age and are not represented through some
male member) a full statement of 'the real and personal estate of the Society.'
In matters of great importance special meetings of the whole Society may
be called. But in general the Society has avoided the mistake (common
enough in many contemporary communities) of too many mass meetings. It
took five upheavals of the Icarian Community to teach the lesson of leaving
routine administration to committees instead of discussing every detail in frequent meetings of the assembly.

"The Amana Society aims to keep its members informed on the general
condition of affairs; but there is a decided tendency to reduce unnecessary
discussion to the minimum by 'leaving such things to those that best understand them.' The Board of Trustees is the high court of appeal in cases of
disagreements, dissension, and complaints within the Society. Owing to the
nature of the Community there are no lawyers in Amana. However, in suits
with outside parties the Society does not hesitate to employ counsel.

"Each village is governed by a group of elders varying in number — not
necessarily old men, but men who are deemed to be of deep piety and spirituality. At the same time the Community profoundly believes that 'Days
should speak and multitude of years should teach wisdom.' By that nice
adjustment of functions that necessarily grows up in such a community, the

highest authority in the village in matters spiritual is the Head Elder; in matters temporal, the resident Trustee. And although the Trustee is a member of the Great Council itself, which is the spiritual head of the Community, in the village church, the Head Elder outranks the Trustee.

"Each village keeps its own books and manages its own affairs in accordance with the resolutions of the Great Council; but all accounts are finally sent to the headquarters at Amana where they are inspected and the balance of profit or loss is discovered. It is presumed that the labor of each village produces a profit; but whether it does or not makes no difference in the supplies allotted to the village or to members thereof. The system of government is thus a sort of federation wherein each village maintains a certain sphere of independence in local administration, but is under the general control and supervision of a governing central authority — the Board of Trustees or Great Council of the Brethren.

"The Amana houses are substantially built, and quite unpretentious. It has been the purpose of the Community to construct the houses as nearly alike as possible. There is no hard and fast rule, but the aim is to make one as desirable as the other. There is in the private homes no kitchen, no dining-room, no parlor — just a series of sitting-rooms and bed-rooms, which are, almost without exception, roomy and homelike. In addition to the general family sitting-room, each member of a household has as a rule his own individual sitting-room as well as his own individual bed-room. Here he is at liberty to indulge his own taste in decoration — provided that he does not go beyond his allowance or violate the rules of the Community. Here he may ride his hobbies or store his keepsakes without being disturbed — which accounts in part for the general content of the young people.

"General housekeeping in Amana is a comparatively simple matter. At more or less regular intervals in each village there is a 'kitchen-house'—a little larger than the ordinary dwelling — where the meals for the families in the immediate neighborhood are prepared and served. From sixteen to fifty persons eat at one kitchen, the number depending largely upon the location. The places are assigned by the resident Trustee or local Council, the chief consideration being the convenience of those concerned.

"The kitchen-house system of Amana may lack the economy of the communistic ideal — the unitary dining-room — but there is much to be said in its favor. To the Great Council of the Brethren the purity and simplicity of the Community have ever been more important considerations than minimum expenditure. * * * Mass meeting is in no way a part of the working scheme of the Amana Society. Even in the church there are separate apartments or meeting-rooms for the young men, the young women, and the older members. Indeed, if Amana has made any distinctive contribution to practical, working communism, it is in the combination, or rather the nice adjustment, between separatism and communism, whereby mutual interest is maintained without inviting the pitfalls of too much getting together.

"The Amana kitchen is large and airy, often extending through the full depth of the house. Each kitchen has its supply of hot and cold water and its sink and drain. Every pan and kettle has its shelf or hook; and there are more conveniences for paring and slicing, chopping and grinding, than the average housewife of the world ever dreamed of. But the really distinctive feature of the Amana kitchen is the long low brick stove with its iron plate top. This is built along one side of the room; and back of it there is a sheet of tin several feet high which shines like a mirror. For its upper edge hangs a most surprising variety of strainers, spoons, dippers, and ladles. On top of the brick stove are the huge copper boilers and kettles which a community kitchen necessitates. In recent years there has been added to each kitchen a modern cook-stove, which is used during the winter for heating as well as for cooking purposes.

"In the kitchen everything from the floor to ceiling is as clean and bright as can be made by soap and water, brooms and mops. The Amana woman knows none of the vexations of the village housewife of the world, in whose home as a rule proper conveniences for the kitchen are the last to be provided. Woodsheds and store-houses are built in the most convenient places; there are covered passage-ways from the house to the 'bake-oven' and outstandings; and there is commonly a hired man at the kitchen-house for the carrying of water and hewing of wood. There is absolute system in every detail of the house work; and the women do not appear to be overworked.

"Each kitchen is superintended by a woman appointed by the Elders, who is assisted by three of the younger women, each taking her turn in attending to the dining-room, preparing vegetables, cooking, and washing dishes. As a general rule, one week of 'part time' follows two weeks of service in the kitchen — which, it must be admitted, is a great improvement over the ceaseless routine of the life of the average housewife of the world. The older women do not work in the kitchen as a rule; hence it is sometimes necessary to hire help from the outside. It is the aim of the Community to have hired help in the hotel kitchens in order to shield its own young women from too close contact with the world. The fact that the average summer visitor too often leaves his manners in the city when he chances to take an outing makes the wisdom of such a rule evident.

"Wagons from the village bakery, butcher shop, and dairy make the daily rounds of the kitchens. Cheese and unsalted butter for table use are made in each kitchen, along with its own special cooking and baking. Large dryers at the woolen mills, where steam heat can be utilized are now used for the drying of vegetables for winter use.

"It is the aim of the Community to produce as far as practicable all the food consumed by the members. At the same time the Amana people do not deny themselves any comforts which are compatible with simplicity of life. The tables are bountifully laden with wholesome food; but the menu is practically the same from day to day, except as varied by the presence of fresh fruits and vegetables in their season. The Inspirationists are not faddists in their diet; they have no theories regarding the effect of a vegetable and fruit diet on 'the health of the body, and the purity of the mind, and the happiness of society.' They have no decided opinions regarding the relative merits of lard and tallow, and no rule against the 'eating of dead creatures.' Tea and coffee are commonly used. In short, the food throughout the Community is well cooked and substantial, but unmodified by any modern dietetic philosophy.

"Breakfast is served in the Amana kitchens at six o'clock in the summer-time and half an hour later in the winter-time. The dinner hour is 11:30 the year 'round. With the supper bell, which rings at half past six in the winter-time and at seven o'clock in the summer-time, the day's work closes. In addition to these three meals the Inspirationist takes a lunch in the middle of each half day. Those who work at considerable distance from the kitchen carry their lunches with them. When the supper things are cleared the members gather in small groups at different places in the villages for the evening prayer-meeting.

"There was a time in the pioneer days of the Community (when all energies were bent to the building of a new home in the wilderness) when the women, in the manner of our Puritan grandmothers, shared almost equally the physical labors of the men. But as the Community prospered the lot of the women became easier; and to-day the woman of Amana knows nothing of the cares of the average house-mother who is expected to perform the combined duties of housemaid and nurse, hostess and church worker.

"In every department of service in which woman participates the work is carefully apportioned to her strength. The woman with children under the age of two is not required to take part in the general village work, and her meals are brought to her home in a basket from the nearest kitchen-house. There is a nursery or kindergarten in each village well supplied with sand piles and the variety of playthings deemed necessary to keep children interested. Here the little folks between three years and school age are cared for when necessary to enable their mothers to take part in the village work.

"In connection with every kitchen-house is a vegetable garden of from two to three acres. The heaviest of the garden work is always done by the hired man; but the superintendence and general care of the garden are entrusted to the women. This work is lighter than the kitchen work and the hours are shorter; and so the garden work is allotted to the middle-aged and older women.

"Whoever has fared on the produce of the kitchen-house garden can understand the feeling of the Amana prodigal who returned to the Community because there was "nothng fit to eat in the world." There is fresh lettuce from March to December, grown in hotbeds at one end of the garden and kept in sand in the cellar at the other. There is ever-green spinach that is delicious the whole summer long; and the garden superintendent knows how to lengthen the green pea and wax bean season to the most surprising extent. There are great white cauliflowers averaging ten inches across; there are kale and salsify, red cabbage and yellow tomatoes, and much more that the visitor from the world does not even know by name. At one end of the summer the kitchen garden brings forth huge strawberries and raspberries, to which even the gorgeously illustrated seed catalogues can not do justice; and at the other end a marvelous variety of apples, and pears, and plums, and grapes.

"Formerly the village tailor made all of the clothing for the men, but it was found to be cheaper to buy 'ready-made' clothes for ordinary wear. The 'best clothes' are still quite generally made by the Community tailor; for the young man gets his goods at cost from the woolen mills, and, as the time cf the tailor belongs to the Society, he is thus enabled to dress well on less than one fourth of what it costs his brother in the world. The older Brothers are a little more orthodox and still wear 'Colony' trousers and a Sunday coat without lapels. * * *

"The costume of the women might almost be called a uniform two hundred years old, the dress of to-day among the more orthodox being practically the same as at the founding of the Community. Until recently the summer clothing of the women was made largely of the calico printed by the Community and known from Maine to California as 'Amana Calico.' The printing works, however, were closed during the World War, owing to the impossibility of obtaining reliable dyes — particularly the indigo for the Society's best known 'Colony Blue' — and up to the present time the industry has not been resumed. The only head dress in the summer time is a sun bonnet with a long cape; a hood takes its place in cold weather.

"The religious services of the Community of True Inspiration are numerous, but extremely simple. There is no attempt at rhetorical effect or eloquence on the part of the Elders; the hymns are chanted without instrumental accompaniment and ofttimes the prayer is 'unhindered by words.' The service is dignified and breathes throughout a reverent and devout spirit, and ever there remains the sincere effort of the forefathers to eliminate all that is formal and bound to the letter. At the close of the service the congregation quietly files out of the church. If it chances to be a general meeting, the women all leave the church by one exit and the men by another. This no doubt is calculated to prevent 'silly conversation and trifling conduct.' There are no greetings, no good-byes, no visiting on the steps of the church — nothing in fact that would tend to lessen the solemnity of the occasion.

"The Community to-day is a living history of all of the work and character and ideals that have been associated with it in the past; and when we look into the faces of the splendid young men and women to whom it has been handed on as a precious inheritance, when we hear the chant of the primer class' as it floats out of the vine-covered school window, we know that in spite of external modifications and adjustments, in spite of the occasional 'emblem of vanity' and 'worldly amusement,' in spite of the inevitable 'black sheep' in the fold, much of the beautiful spirit of 'the old defenders of the faith' still pervades the Community. The history of mankind teaches that 'religion often makes practicable that which were else impossible, and divine love triumphs when human science is baffled.' "

BERTHA M. H. SHAMBAUGH.

BOTANY BAY MUTINEERS
1825 to Present Time

One of the strangest of all communities was that of the Bounty Mutineers, established in the early part of the nineteenth century. A group of seamen, with some officers, mutinied and fled from the British warship Bounty, commanded by Admiral Bligh, disarming those who failed to go with them. The mutineers set forth in open boats, evidently with some hazy notion of becoming Captain Kidds. They first landed on the Marquesian Islands, one of the Polynesian group, where each man took a woman. They soon departed with the women. It is not recorded by what means they induced the women to leave—whether they were taken in battle or by barter or by mutual consent. Staying below the tropic of Capricorn, the mutineers finally landed on a rugged island which they called Pitt, after one of their leaders, a Scotchman. It reminded the latter of his native rocky land, so he added the "cairn," meaning rocks, to it.

Whether or not the island was inhabited prior to their coming is not known. If so, it was by Melanesians, who are the negroid type of South sea Islanders, and distinctly inferior to the Polynesians, who are known as the "Aristocrats of the human race." Any negroid Melanesians would probably have been killed by the invaders. At this time the latter, with the women, numbered between 50 and 60, and among them were several naval officers.

The mutiny had been in the vicinity of the Hawaiian Islands, and as no trace of the mutineers was ever found, it was assumed that they had been lost in a storm. Not until 25 years later were they discovered on Pitcairn Island. During this period, as a result of the American Revolution, the system of expatriating prisoners had been changed, and now they were being put on islands in the vicinity of Australia. In time Pitcairn Island was found, and to the intense surprise of the discoverers, a thriving community was found.

Among the islands selected for prisoners were Norfolk and Tasmania. Norfolk, under Governor Burgess, became a place of plenty. It is only six miles wide and ten miles long, and the beauty-loving governor had it laid out like an English garden, with a border of trees around the entire island.

But eventually the British government found that putting prisoners on the mainland of Australia was preferable to maintaining the island prisons, and Norfolk was abandoned. Because of the stigma which had been attached to it, no one could be found who was willing to live on it.

Meantime the sons and grandsons of the Bounty Mutineers had multiplied. The island of Pitcairn was overcrowded. Instead of being considered as outcasts, these newly-discovered British-Polynesian subjects of the Queen were looked upon as very lovable wards, and finally Norfolk Island was tendered them. They gladly accepted it, thus becoming heirs to many fine buildings and an island which was not only beautiful, but which had been brought to a high point of productiveness.

During the time they were on Pitcairn, and because of the exigencies of their position, or perhaps because they learned something from their Polynesian wives, the Pitcairn Islanders developed community living, holding all goods in common and benefitting on an equality from their associated industry. This system of community living they took with them to Norfolk Island. Some of the Pitcairn Islanders were also sent to Lord Howe Island. But all maintained their community living, though they eventually adopted different religions, some becoming Episcopalians, and other Seventh Day Adventists.

Soon after taking up residence on Norfolk they grew slothful and lazy and sought the easiest lines of making a living. The making of liquor was developed, and for a time they were in danger of extinction because of their drunkenness. Eventually there arose one John Fletcher who took charge and saved them, inducing them to again go back to their industrious habits.

The British government has permitted these integral co-operators to have their own system of government, though it sends a judge among them and perhaps some other officers.

With a whole island, productive and rich, with a perfect climate, with splendid buildings, and with everything they need, these co-operators are rich. They use no money, and the richest man among them had about $25. They barter mostly. But they are rich, nevertheless, for they have all of the means of producing all they need or want, and they have no fear of losing this wealth. They have security and happiness.

Although some community dwellers have become pacifists, these Norfolk Islanders have not; and they are fanatically loyal to Great Britain, as perhaps they have good reason to be, for certainly they are beneficiaries of the government their ancesters deserted. During the war they pledged most of their chattels to the government.

There are probably four hundred people on Norfolk Island, the chief one of the group of community islands now owned by the descendants of the would-be buccaneers of the good ship Bounty, deserted by a part of her crew more than a century ago. But whatever may have been their ideals or lack of them or their misdeeds or wrong intentions, they were forced into a system of living which has made them safe and secure and which has won for their children's children a greater measure of happiness and safety and security and material wealth than falls to the majority of people anywhere.

THE PERFECTIONIST COMMUNITIES
1848 to Present Time

One of the best-known communities is the Oneida Community, tho few know that it was purely communistic in its early history, and only when its industries outgrew the colony was it incorporated and its industries conducted as a purely commercial enterprise, chief among them being the famous Community Silver, widely advertised.

Before the Oneida Community, however, was the Putney Community, with its history really a part of the latter as the Oneida Community was in effect a continuation of the Putney. John Humphrey Noyes, Perfectionist leader and preacher, founded both of them, and also Wallingford and all were successful. Deeply religious, he became a critic of religions at an early age and refused to be confined by existing religious fetters. He later aided in the organization of one of the earliest Anti-Slavery Societies and devoted much time to religious work among colored people.

Noyes tried to make himself a perfect Christian, and on one occasion claimed a degree of perfection that won for him and his followers, eventually, the title Perfectionists. He was ordained for the ministry, but would not conform to the teachings and requirements of the Yale Theological Seminary and finally lost his license to preach because of heresy. He finally returned to his father's home in Putney, Vermont. There, with his wife, his two brothers and two sisters, and the wife of one of the brothers, a community was formed consecrated to religion. All things were possessed in common. A farm came to the brothers in settlement of the father's estate and another to the two sisters, and were turned into the little colony. The work of publishing a little paper was done by the small community. This was in 1838. A year later several additional members joined. Gradually others joined, many of them skilled in trades. In 1845 the association was organized and called the Putney Corporation.

The officers were to be a president and a secretary and three directors. At least three of the five must agree on any measure; in the event of disagreement the matter might be submitted to the group. The unanimous consent of the members of the corporation was required for the admission of new members. Any member could withdraw at any time by notifying the Board of Officers and assuming his own maintenance. Any member could be excluded from the corporation by a vote of a majority of the members. All property belonging to the members at the time of subscribing to the constitution or which they might subsequently come into possession of, was to be held as the property of the corporation, subject to the control of the executive officers.

A school was early established at which Hebrew, Greek, Latin, and other branches were taught. The group possessed 500 acres of good land, seven dwellings, a store, printing shop, and other buildings. The members occupied separate homes, but lived as a family. The hope of the community was that it might some day publish a daily religious paper.

One of the features of the Putney community was the belief in miraculous healing. One of the members, known to the villagers for years as an invalid, sick with a complication of diseases, nearly blind, pronounced to be incurable, and expected to die at any time, was "raised instantly by the laying on of hands and by the word of command * * *" This caused great excitement. The woman's husband, an avowed infidel, previously not attracted to the Perfectionists, testified that his wife had been raised by the power of God, and that the same power had raised him from the darkness and misery of unbelief. This, together with the social innovations of the Perfectionists, was the excuse for indignation meetings and a denunciation of Noyes and his associates. Perhaps the social innovations were the collective marriages. Legal proceedings were threatened. The paper was voluntarily suspended, and Mr. Noyes left Putney, the others following soon. Less than three years later a sub-colony of the Oneida Community was established in Putney and was maintained for five years.

ONEIDA

A few months later, those who had fled from Putney, with some of those who had remained in Putney, gathered at Oneida, with a membership on January, 1849, of 87 members. During the year the membership doubled; in February, 1851, there were 205 members, in 1875 there were 298 members in Oneida Community and its branches, and in 1878 there were 306. It will be seen that the growth was not rapid, for in nearly 30 years the growth was only from 87 to 306, an average gain of less than 8 persons a year. Walingford and some others were established in the early 50's; but soon the policy of concentration was adopted, and the financial prosperity of the community dates from this time.

At first the Oneida Community consisted of two small frame dwellings, a log hut, and an old sawmill, once owned by the Indians. It was a dozen years before the members got beyond sleeping in garrets and out-houses. The industries were of the simplest and rudest—farming, logging, milling, clearing swamps—and in this work, particularly the latter, the women took part, as they did in the later home-building. There were no distinctions of classes in respect to labor. The Community treasury was frequently empty and at times they could not pay postage. Grocery bills remained unpaid at times and the larder was lean. During the first nine years of pioneer work the community reduced its capital from $107,000 to $67,000, but it improved its organization, developed important principles and measures, and started several businesses, some of which proved fairly remunerative. Gradually the Community won the esteem of neighbors and others.

Visitors were attracted from everywhere and at times as many as 1000 to 1500 persons thronged the grounds.

Most of the Perfectionists were Americans. There were some well-educated men and women among them. Women worked in the industries. The community hired some outside labor. They permitted women to take up any occupations they desired. In 1880 the hired employes numbered from one hundred to two hundred and fifty. Though not in sympathy with the system of paying wages, they did this in the hope that they were helping those who could not understand collectivism.

Superintendents were appointed after being freely discussed by officials and lay members. The Business Board elected some. This Board was composed of all members who cared to attend its sessions. A number of department managers were appointed or elected, heading the departments of trap-making, silk-working, fruit-packing, and other work.

The system of complex marriage, by which each man was married to all of the women and each woman to all of the men, which had been severely criticised, gave rise to a community system of caring for children. These were regarded as children of the community and brought up together on that footing. The dietary was simple and wholesome, and the children were usually healthy. They had large playrooms and community nurses interested in their work. Children were weaned at nine months and then placed in the Children's House and cared for by nurses serving half-day shifts, being returned to the mothers at five o'clock. They were taken to the House again at 8:00 the next morning. Mothers were not separated from their children, but they were relieved of the care of them and given a freedom that mothers do not usually have.

The Oneida community had a library of 6000 volumes, and kept many magazines on file. It had a play house for the children. Amusements in the colony were subject to only such restrictions as were required by good order. There was a summer resort at Oneida Lake, 12 miles distant, and another on Long Island Sound. At one time the Community had 650 acres of good land, with pasturage, orchards, vineyards, gardens, and a cannery. Among the occupations pursued were shoemaking, tailoring, dentistry, printing, carpentering, and other trades; but the chief business enterprises were the canning of fruit and vegetables, the manufacture of silk, and the making of traps. Much reliance was placed on a peculiar system known as Mutual Criticism, which originated in a secret society of missionary brethren with which Mr. Noyes was connected when a student. In the Oneida Community it became a principal means of discipline and government. There was a standing committee of criticism, selected by the community and changed from time to time, thus giving all an opportunity to serve both as critics and subjects. The subject was free to have others besides the critics present if he wished. The members of the Oneida Community said of it:

"It is not easy to overestimate the usefulness of criticism in its relation to community life. There is hardly a phase of that life in which it does not play an important part. It is the regulator of industry and amusement—the incentive to all improvement—the corrector of all excesses. It governs and guides ,all. Criticism, in short, bears nearly the same relation to Communism that the system of judicature bears to ordinary society. As society cannot exist without government, and especially without a sysem of courts and police, so Communism requires for its best development free mutual criticism."

The Oneida Community had another ordinance which they regarded as. being of great importance to their harmony and general progress. This was the Daily Evening Meetings, an hour in length, conducted with little formality. Matters of business, of community order and government, the news of the day, scientific discussion, home lectures, religious testimony and discourse, music, and everything of common interest came in for its share of attention.

The community had no definite regulations respecting hours of rising and of labor, leaving such matters for the most part to the judgment and inclination of the individual members. They had little trouble from the shiftless and the lazy. Where reproof or counsel was needed, it was given thru their system of criticism already described.

The Oneida Communists, like the Shakers, Harmonists, and other Collectivists, were long-lived. Many lived to be over four score years and 22 died between 85 and 96. They gave much attention to hygienic conditions, living on simple food and following after temperance in all things.

Though the Community claimed that its system was founded on religion, and they had little faith in the success of any system of Communism which had not a religious basis, yet they were practical rather than theological religionists and were far from being mere formalists. They were not afraid that religion would suffer from any truth which science might discover, and the works of Huxley, Tyndall, and Darwin and Spencer were well represented in their library. They encouraged education, art, music, amusement, and everything which tends to human culture and happiness.

The Oneida Community won the respect of all. A citizen of Oneida, but not of the Community, wrote to a Syracuse paper:

"The Oneida Community members are extremely polite, gentlemanly in dress and manners, using no profane or vulgar language, no cigars, tobacco, or whiskey, are never sued and never sue any one, furnish no cases for the police court, have no paupers and no bastard children. Every department of their business is a model of neatness and order."

In 1879 Mr. Noyes asked the Community to act on certain modifications of their rules and regulations. Reasons given were, among others, that children growing up in the Community had not the intense religious convictions of their parents. There had been much criticism, especially in religious circles, of the social radicalism of the members of the Community.

Those proposals were:

1—That the practice of Complex Marriages be given up, not as renouncing belief in the principles, but in deference to public opinion.

2—That the members of the Community be of two distinct classes—the married and the celibates—with preference to the latter group.

3—That all property and business be held in common as formerly.

4—That they continue to live together in a common household and all to eat at a common table.

5—That a common children's department be conducted as previously.

6—That the daily evening meetings be continued as a means of moral and spiritual improvement.

The message by Mr. Noyes was considered and adopted a week later, which made great changes in their institution and profoundly impressed many of the members. This change was made on August 26, 1879. Twenty marriages followed during the rest of the year. Scarcely half a dozen celibates remained.

The next important change was from community interest in property to a joint stock corporation with shares representing individual holdings. After sixteen months of study and deliberation the change was made. About twenty went to California and others to Boston and New York, so that a disintegration of community life followed the social and business changes. No efforts were made to form other communities.

The method of apportioning the interests in the community was to give each and all, without regard to sex, service, or usefulness, four shares of stock, valued at $100 each for every year of membership, and half the money put in by members refunded in shares. An alternative offer was an annuity of $200 with guarantee for care in sickness and some other considerations; but only two persons accepted this. Children were guaranteed from $80 to $120 a year (as profits allowed) and eight months of schooling until sixteen years of age, at which time each was given $200 outright. This division proved satisfactory and there were no complaints.

"The benefits to character from long communal training," says Mr. Hinds, "was shown." Had any demanded in full the money put in, this division would not have been possible and many aged members might not have received property which left them independent in their old age. As might have been expected, persons who had left the Community dmanded a part of the property and six sought to enforce claims through the courts, but failed to establish cause for action. These suits cost the Community $10,000.

"Financially the new company has been successful," says Mr. Hinds,

Beginning in 1881 with a paid-up capital of $600,000, it has distributed quarterly dividends averaging six per cent per annum, and accumulated a considerable surplus. On March 1, 1907, the capital stock of the Oneida Community, Limited, was $1,200,000, with a surplus of $112,000, making a total of $1,312,000.00. In addition to this, there was a special capital of deposit accounts of members, employes, etc., approximating $392,000."

Altho the Oneida Community voluntarily gave up its communal features, it demonstrated conclusively the progress, the benefits, the advantages, and the beauties of such a life. The years of growth were slow and painful, but the material rewards in later years were great. From every point of view the Oneida Community may be regarded as highly successful.

A letter from J. H. Noyes, secretary of the Oneida Community, Limited, shows the amazing prosperity of this enterprise since Mr. Hinds wrote of it in 1907, and also shows how ownership has remained largely in the hands of the descendants of the original Communists:

Ernest S. Wooster   April 21, 1924.
Leesville, Louisiana,

Dear Sir:—In reply to yours of the 18th the changes which have taken place in the Company's affairs since the date of Mr. Hinds' book, 1908, are chiefly such as would attend the steady growth of a concern of large calibre. At that time the total capital stock was $1,200,000, all common stock. The present authorized capital is $7,000,000, of which over $5,300,000 is outstanding. There was a common stock-dividend of 50% in 1913, a small one of 6¼% in 1913 and another of 12½% this year.

We enclose annual statement as of January 31, 1924, which gives details of condition. You will note there were no bank loans whatever.

It may be said that the management is quite largely in the hands of the descendants of the former community, and that over 80% of the common stock is held by former community people, their children, and by a considerable group of workers in the industrial organizations who were not former members, but who have been in the employ of the company for many years.

Sincerely,

J. H. NOYES, Secretary.

Statement of condition as at January 31, 1924, shows assets as follows:

Plant—Land and Buildings; Machinery; Home and
    Industrial Housing and Equipment.....................................$2,931,950.93
Securities and other Assets; Inventories; Accounts
    Receivable; Cash, etc..$5,028,306.12
                      TOTAL.....................................$7,960,257.05

The following excerpts from an article by C. C. Church, "Critic and Guide" of May, 1924, are of interest:

"The Oneida Community began as a retreat from the Calvinism and

Puritanism reigning so largely in New England a century ago. Some of its members were linked with the leading families of Vermont, and the group of over two hundred people were, evidently, a well-assorted lot. They brought with themselves to this 'sortie or raid from the kingdom of God' into the world a respectable amount of wealth, about four hundred dollars per capita.

"Perfectionists, believing in their own perfectability, even before they were communists, they set about to create circumstances conducive to salvation from sin. Mystics of indigenous growth, they were too canny to neglect their environment. Presently, by modes of organization the new communists conquered the pain of labor. Their workday was short, sometimes of only six hours. Each producing member secured variety by moving easily from one occupation to another. The commingling of the sexes in the industries of the group, the men performing the heavier tasks, added a pleasant feature. Co-operative methods and a very modern dormitory abolished household drudgery. Being successful, the communism permitted each person to taste a delightful freedom from care. Therefore, according to the Handbook of the Oneida Community, there were no shirkers to reckon with. Little wonder, then, that, while conducting propaganda and fighting persecution, the society added notably to its wealth so that it was called rich by its observers. However, it boasted not of its riches, but of its happy living.

"By a sexual order known as 'complex marriage' this idyllic society attempted to fit sexuality for a well-groomed appearance in the Holy City itself. Thus the community became famous.

"But a certain control, male continence, in sexual behavior was mandatory, both parties must desire a union, advances were made through third parties, and every secret place of the heart was penetrated by the piercing rays of an institution known as 'mutual criticism.' In little meetings the last hidden motive and thought of each member was tested for righteousness. If there was anything gross in the sexual attitudes of these people the Freudian censor certainly saw that it was well-disguised. The ideal was a refinement of life according to apostolic Christianity.

"The exemplary public behavior of the communists served as a partial antidote for their iconoclasm. They were wholesomely industrious and squarely honest. They abstained from liquor, tobacco, profanity, and fashions in dress. They despised obscenity. The fact that the community almost entirely escaped venereal disease is attributable in part to the chaste attitude towards outsiders. Some new adherents after joining the society found themselves more willing to partake of its privileges than to do their part in creating these. Such persons on leaving the community were usually given their original contribution, or, if they had contributed nothing, one hundred dollars. These payments were made, however, not as matters of right, but of liberality, and no claims for wages were allowed. As these conditions were always made known to prospective members, they looked fair.

"Because the Perfectionist group claimed with some show of evidence to be an ideal home of harmony, the churches retaliated by claiming that it was an asylum of vice and the epitome of arrogance. Newspaper men and journalists, like Frank Leslie, true to a bent not uncommon in their guilds, wrote salacious accounts of the experiment.

"An important obstacle to the orthodox clergy in their assault on the community was the absence of any laws to prevent it doing as it was doing; it was not illegal, never having been anticipated by statute-makers. When the enemies of complex marriage were about at the point of getting special legislation passed in their favor, the communists took counsel. Other communities, less offensive, had been stripped by lawyers of a little wealth once accumulated. The Oneida Community would not permit itself to be robbed of what its children and aged deserved. Resistance to the state government would be criminal. Therefore, in August, 1879, the society formally withdrew from the practice of complex marriage, although a belief in the principle was reasserted.

KORESHAN UNITY
1889 to Present Time

Cyrus R. Teed, founder of the Koreshan Unity at Estero, Florida, about 1889, was a physician who claimed to be a prophet under control of supernal forces. The Persian form of Cyrus is Koresh, and this is the name which he gave to the religion, calling it Koreshanity, which was to supplant Christianity. A part of his creed was a belief in Communism, and this is the material basis of the group at Estero, Florida. The city was incorporated with 110 miles of territory, which was to provide for the immense number of converts expected. At one time a following of 10,000 was claimed, with 200 persons in the colony. The city was laid out to be a magnificent world center, but has not grown materially in numbers, nor have the expected improvements been made. The celibate conditions imposed have had the usual deterrent effect. The community is conducted in much the same way that many of the religious communities have been conducted, except that it has not had the vigor or energy to produce, much of the living having always come from the outside instead of having been produced from within.

Peter Hanson, a member of the Llano Colony, but for some years a member of the Koreshan Unity, had little to add to the account given by Hinds as regards the colony, which reached its zenith some years ago. The account furnished by Mr. Hanson claimed that there were 200 residents, and that the value of the property was a quarter of a million dollars, tho this included some items not usually considered as quick assets. There were 7000 acres of land. Much attention was given to education, and this includes musical education. Boys were taught trades. This was a description of conditions in 1908. Mr. Hanson adds:

"Since then the colony has been on a decline, some of the property has been lost, and the membership has been reduced to about 70. The colony is dormant, like a seed before it sprouts. The fact that it has held together the last 16 years against self-seekers, and against all kinds of odds under which other organizations would not have lasted a week speaks well for the cohesive elements so necessary in a colony. Koresh declared himself to be a preparer of the way for the New Order; his personal mission was completed in 1892. * * * When the destructive forces of capital and labor have destroyed each other, the New Order will be established." Mr. Hanson is still an enthusiastic believer in the creed and in the other principles of Koreshanity, though not now a resident of the community.

However, a letter from another ex-member must also be considered. This man is no admirer of the Unity. In the absence of an authentic statement by a member of the Unity, the compiler of this volume has been compelled to rely on such sources as he was able to reach, and the letter from which quotations are given below was not friendly in its expressions.

"The first convert was a Mr. Dampkohler, who had 320 acres at Estero. Teed promised Dampkohler all things * * * Finally Dampkohler sued Teed and the lawyers compromised, leaving Teed 160 acres and the balance was absorbed by the lawyers, leaving Dampkohler nothing * * * There must have been thousands of people who have passed thru the colony since then. The present membership is 51 voters and perhaps 10 children. Fifteen years ago they had 200, and I think that is the highest number. They now hold about 2000 acres; in 1908 they had 7000, but lost 4000 by foreclosure. They paid $12,000 for worthless, mostly overflowed, land. No industries have been conducted with any semblance of sanity. The only ones now paying are a shop in which they charge all the traffic will bear, and the printery by which they issue their Flaming Sword * * * Only a few members come now, possibly two or three a year."

However, the Koreshans proved themselves heroic in the matter of staying with their community thru hardships. The same correspondent tells of their living on cornmeal mush and corn bread, and not enough of it, for months at a time. Koresh was absolute ruler, and his word was not questioned. A complaint made against him was that he lived in luxury at at times when the other members of the Unity lived in extremely moderate circumstances, though Hinds says that Victoria, his associate, lived in extreme poverty with the others. Even the one who wrote in bitterness admits that the property now owned is worth about $200,000, though there are few improvements, and none of any considerable value. They publish another paper also, the American Eagle, but it is not a propaganda paper.

Of chief interest, however, is the theory upon which this colony is founded. It is known as Cellular Cosmogeny. It admits that the earth is round, but asserts that we live inside of it instead of outside. Their literature says:

"The fundamental premise of the Copernican system of astronomy is the hypothesis that the surface of the earth on which we live is convex. The well-known phenomenon of the disappearance of a ship's hull beyond the horizon of the surface of the sea is one of the principal so-called proofs offered in support of the popular theory; it is constantly being urged as an objection to the Koreshan conclusion that the earth is a hollow globe, with its habitable surface concave instead of convex. If the usual theory were true, specific tests would verify it; as it is fallacious, ocular tests are sufficient to disprove it and to overthrow the entire system.

In order to appreciate the value and force of such experiments of observation as have been conducted during the past few years by the Koreshan Scientific Staff, it is necessary to consider the ratio of the earth's curvature, and the claims of the advocates of the old school of astronomy. We desire to examine the subject just as it is presented by the astronomer, and subject the theory to the test of the facts of observation. The so-called proof is an ocular one, used hundreds of years before the invention of the telescope; and it is but fair, in a scientific age, to submit it to ocular test, with the power of vision increased by telescope aid.

"If the surface of the sea were convex, the water line of the horizon would be the simple apex of the arc of the water's curvature. If the hull of a vessel disappeared on a rotund surface, it would do so because of the simple fact that it had passed to a point below the visual line extending from the eye over the apex or horizon. In other words, the hull would be rendered absolutely invisible by the intervening hill of water. We desire to state the question fairly, so that there can be no quibbling concerning the premise upon which the old system is made to rest.

"A convex earth 25,000 miles in circumference would have a curvature of 8 inches to the mile, or, according to the geometrical formula, the square of the distance in miles, multiplied by 8 inches, gives the declination in inches, from the tangent line. In two miles the curvature downward from the tangent would be 32 inches; 3 miles, 6 feet; 4 miles, 10 feet and 8 inches; 8 miles, 42 feet and 8 inches * * *.

"On August 27, 1899 a target 3 feet broad and 6 feet in length was suspended over the wall constituting the base of the lighthouse on the new Government pier, Chicago; the bottom of the target just touched the water. A 4½-foot mounted telescope, with 3-inch object glass, was placed at an elevation of 11 feet above the water, on the pier at the old World's Fair grounds, a little over 8 miles south of the lighthouse. To the unaided eye at 11 feet elevation, about one third of the lighthouse tower appeared to be below the horizon; only the tops of the engine-houses could be seen above the water line. The new Government pier itself was entirely invisible. Yachts in the vicinity of the lighthouse appeared about half sail "down."

"Now, we meet the so-called proof of the earth's convexity squarely face to face. Is it true or not? If it is true, when we view the lighthouse thru the telescope, from the same elevation as with the naked eye, no part of the objects apparently below the horizon can be seen; only as much of the tower as stands above the line B in the diagram we have referred to, would appear in the telescopic field; it would be physically impossible for it to be otherwise. The telescope was directed to the lighthouse; a clear focus was obtained, and careful views, extending over a period of three hours, were witnessed by about fifty persons who were present on the pier. We saw the tower to the line B; the wall of masonry at the base of the tower, and the target below B down to the water's surface. The action of the waves against the wall was clearly observed.

"The target was a special one, with horizontal stripes of red and white. We counted the stripes on the target to definitely ascertain whether or not we observed the whole of it; there was not a square foot of it invisible!

Yachts sailing about the pier, appearing half mast "down" to the naked eye, were visible, hulls and all, down to the surface on which they sailed. * * *

"Immortality depends upon the conservation of the pneumic and psychic energies of being, and their direction and appropriation thru scientific determinations of the mind, dependent upon the wisdom of the Shepherd or Messiah of this age, who will lead the sheep of the fold.

"We have no room for those who cannot recognize the Messianic law; especially, have we no room in the interior orders of our institution. Our literature sufficiently sets forth our religious and social principles, so as to leave no misapprehension of what we teach. We have now two distinct local divisions of our headquarters; one in Estero, Florida, and one in Chicago. Our publishing house is located in Chicago. Our Capitol City is Estero, but remotely a developed Capitol. People coming to us in Estero come to a "simon-pure" pioneer life, one of strenuosity and sacrifice. We have people, educated and refined, who have left the attractions of the worldly existence and are happy in the life chosen here. We have those who have been through the severest features of this pioneer work for eight or nine years, and are still happy in their efforts to plant for future generations the habitation of liberty.

"Our institution is one of common interest. We hold all things in common; and so far as financial claim is concerned, there is no difference between one who has placed one penny in the common treasury, and the one who has contributed one hundred thousand. No person joining our community can claim anything upon the basis of having contributed a large amount of substance to the treasury of the commonwealth. We find the commonwealth idea a more practical and cheerful incentive to industry than the satanic system of competism which, in opposition to the gospel of the Lord Christ, now holds universal sway, and is at the foundaton of all the woe, misery, and death in the world. The commonwealth system obviates "the love of money," which is "the root of all evil."

"We are in no sense socialists after the order of modern socialism. Socialism is individualism; Koreshanity is imperialism. Nor do we hold all things in common upon the basis of equality, for equality does not belong to the order of life in any domain of the universe. Our system presupposes the possibility of an equitable adjustment of education, industry, and commerce, founded upon the laws of order as they obtain in every department of being. All people coming into the institution are expected to abide the issues of progress in the body to adjust according to compatibility and adaptation.

"Modern socialism is entirely theoretical and experimental. It assumes that because kingdoms and democracies have failed to meet the requirements of the age, in such an adjustment of the race as to supply its wants and insure its happiness, the institution of socialism will answer the end in view. Socialism as an experiment would prove a disastrous failure, because it is an attempt to place society upon a basis which is entirely contrary to the laws of order as they obtain in the universe as a whole. Socialism is the insanity of democracy.

"There are certain sociological facts with which we are familiar, because we have put the principles into operation and know that they will work. We are practicing ownership of our land by the state—we mean the state of the Koreshan Unity—and we attained this pre-eminence directly, not through the roundabout way of the single tax principle. We knew that the direct way was the better way, and applied it. Our state owns its land. We have already practically demonstrated the possibility of collective ownership of the land. We pursue our system of commerce on the line of the same principle. We conduct our industrial system on the basis of collective, not individual, propriety.

"We have placed ourselves in contiguity with the greatest channel of international commerce, namely the waterways of the world, that we may take immediate advantage of the most vital avenues of commercial life. Agriculture is the function of the liver; commerce is the function of the heart. We do not buy from or sell to one another; therefore there is no cost as pertaining to our own transactions. We have annihilated the principles of labor, cost, and price, and have no use for the terms in our transactions with one another. That there may be no misunderstanding with such as desire to entertain the question of a trial of our system, we will state that we are in the pioneer stage of our development; that we have not yet reduced labor to a luxury, for our people are performing some drudgery; but they are doing it cheerfully, in the expectation that in the near future our principles will have attained to a degree of fruition.

"We are celibate in doctrine and life; we are communistic in our possession of property; we are obedient to all state and municipal authority: but we advocate a peaceable revolution in the administration of human affairs, knowing that the time is near at hand when the people will be reinstated in their rights; when the governments of the world shall yield authority to the King of kings and Lord of lords, who is the blessed and only Potentate, and who cometh speedily to reign in the earth.

"There are certain steps necessary for permanent connection with the Ecclesia. As a rule, members remain six months in the outer Court—the Investigative degree of the Society Arch-Triumphant. During this time it is expected that the ordinary vices, if obtaining with the person desiring to progress in all the degrees of ethical culture, will have been overcome. We mean profanity, the use of intoxicants and tobacco, and other vices not mentioned but generally understood. When people come into our body with the claim that they have left all and followed the divine teaching, that "all" signifies all that the term implies. To leave all is to sacrifice everything pertaining to the individual loves, and to so revolutionize the love that it will pertain to the general uses rather than to personal desire as founded upon individual and selfish loves.

"When a family comes into the Koreshan Unity, it comes with the understanding that there is a separation; that the children no longer belong to the parents, but to the institution, and that the Unity claims the right to direct the education, industry, and care of the children exclusively, without any regard to what the parents may suppose to be the right thing. The male children belong to the institution until they are twenty-one, and the female children until they are eighteen. This limit is the one placed by law, and all children should be taught that they belong to the Unity and not to their parents. This is a fundamental principle of transposition from the sensual nature to the immortal plane of being.

"Families desiring to enter our organization should first send for cards of application to membership in the Unity. Their initiation is first into the Society Arch-Triumphant. They are supposed to enter upon a probationary period of six months. This allows time for consideration and acquaintance with our principles. We do not always compel applicants to remain out of the body until the expiration of this probation, for sometimes our acquaintance with those who wish to associate with us enables us to insure them an earlier entrance into full fellowship. By a direct action of the Ecclesia, under circumstances warranting it, members can be admitted at once. Moral character, religious proclivities, devotion to humanity, and other considerations, are regarded where direct entrance to the Ecclesia is a question of concern.

"If you enter the Communistic Order, all you possess goes into the treasury of the community—whether it be labor or accumulated wealth in possession before you come to us. You share equally in the wealth of the order with every member. If by communistic fellowship there is amassed a great accumulation of wealth, you are equal possessor of that accumulation. It is a great mistake for one to imagine that if he gives up wealth to the order, the favor is all on one side; that one makes himself poor, while making the society rich. If your preference lies in the direction of the marital or the co-operative order, so express your preference, and your case will considered by the proper authority.

CHRISTIAN COMMUNITY OF UNIVERSAL BROTHERHOOD

DOUKHOBOURS

Previously in Russia; In America 1899 to Present Time

The Doukhobours (Spirit-Wrestlers) have made one of the most successful demonstrations in co-operative colonization and community life of all peoples. Moreover, their colonies are among the largest ever established. They well deserve study by all who are interested in communities, for not only their technique but also their sterling principles give them a deserved place near the head of the list. Not all may agree with the rather low esteem in which they hold education, but few can quarrel with the spirit of their institution. Perhaps their experience justifies the small value they place on education, and a more favorable experience might cause them to change their views.

From a small volume entitled "The Message of the Doukhobours," compiled by Alexander M. Evalenko and used by the "Christians of the Universal Brotherhood," as the Doukhobours frequently call themselves, we take the following:

Vladimir Tchertkoff says of their martyrdom in Russia:

"The Doukhobours first appeared in the middle of the 18th century and soon their numbers had so greatly increased that the Government and the Church, considering the sect to be peculiarly obnoxious, started a cruel persecution. The foundation of the Doukhobours' teaching consists in the belief that the Spirit of God is present in the soul of man, and directs him by its word within him. They understand the coming of Christ in the flesh * * * The whole teaching of the Doukhobours is penetrated with the gospel of love. * * * On fixed days they assemble for prayer meetings at which they read prayers and sing hymns or psalms as they call them, and greet each other fraternally with low bows, thereby acknowledging every man as a bearer of the Divine Spirit. * * *

"The Doukhobours found alike their mutual relations and their relations to other people—and not only to people but to all living creatures—exclusively on love, and therefore they hold all people equal. * * * They consider murder, violence, and in general all relations to living beings not based on love as opposed to their conscience and to the will of God. They are industrious and abstemious in their lives and always truthful in speech, accounting lying a great sin."

Their persecutions began in the latter part of the 18th century. Emperor Alexander said in 1816: "All the measures of severity exhaused upon the Spirit-Wrestlers during the thirty years up to 1801 not only did not destroy this sect, but more and more multiplied the number of its adherents."

Later many were transported to Tiflis, which was thought to be an almost sterile district. However, they flourished and became prosperous there. They amassed wealth, but one of their number, conspiring with officials, betrayed them and seized much of their wealth. Some had been conscripted into the army, but now the majority of the 12,000 Doukhobours took a firm stand against military service, and to this they have remained true ever since. They also burned all of their arms, so no participation in violence became possible.

New persecutions broke out again later. Many of the sect were killed, and large numbers were imprisoned, flogged, and tortured. Disease took many as a consequence of deportations. Large numbers of them were distributed, a family to a village, in hostile districts.

An instance of their extreme non-resistance is related. A Doukhobour heard some one at his barn. He ran out and saw a man about ready to mount a horse and gallop away. "Stop, stop!" he called, and his persuasive tones compelled obedience. The Georgian who was about to steal the horse was told: "I only wanted to tell you that you need not be afraid, and that you should not consider this horse as a stolen one; if you want to take it, do so." The thief did not take the horse.

In 1897 the Doukhobours got an opportunity to present a petition to the Empress of Russia explaining their sufferings and asking to be permitted to settle elsewhere or to emigrate. Friends in England and America assisted, particularly Leo Tolstoy and the Quakers and V. Tchertkoff. Money was raised so that eventually, after staying for some years on the island of Cyprus, the Doukhobours landed in Canada.

On January 23, 1899, 2100 Doukhobours arrived in Halifax, and four days later 1974 more arrived. A large party of men went at once to cut timber for storehouses and dwellings and to prepare for the others. Many went to work on the railroads, turning their wages into the society.

The New York Evening Sun on September 1, 1912, published an account of the Doukhobours from which the following is taken:

"It is ten years now since the Canadian government gave the Doukhobours 320,000 acres of land which at the very lowest valuation must be worth $30 an acre now. True to their co-operative principles, the Doukhobours cultivated one great tract at the center of the land allotted to them, 2000 homesteads of 160 acres each, equal to 15 acres for each settler. When they came to ask for their titles, they did not ask for individual patents, but for the whole piece. They surely met the spirit and the object of the law, but there was no provision made in the law, the authorities said, for the communal method of cultivation, combining so many quarter-sections into one huge tract of property. So the authorities held up their title and finally came forward with a thinly-veiled ultimatum to either become British subjects or else forfeit the land. The Doukhobours gave up the land without a moment's hesitation.

"The Doukhobours retained their freedom and fifteen acres a homestead. It was nothing new for them to contend with official coercion. * * * About 2000 of them remained on what was left of their land and the others went far off into British Columbia, where they purchased 10,000 acres at the junction of the Columbia and Kootenay rivers.

"They will have no police, for there is no crime among them * * * They will not have anything to do with officials except pay their taxes * * *Says a noted Quaker: 'A people who will not fight or steal or drink anything intoxicating, or smoke or use profane language or lie, have a character which will bring forth the best qualities of Christian citizenship.'

"In connection with the sawmills, where also all lumber needed for the buildings is turned out, there is a planing mill. Finished lumber is made there and mouldings; all furniture, tables, and chairs used in the houses are made by their labor. An enormous pumping plant is now nearing completion. When this plant is in working order, the fields will be covered by a network of pipes. In connection with the pumping plant, a generating station will be built to supply light and power to the whole colony. System and co-ordination of effort permeate the whole existence of the Doukhobour communities; everything is done upon joint consideration; no labor is wasted in single-handed effort, and none is undertaken unless the requisite number of hands can be put on the job to effect the maximum saving of time coupled with highest efficiency. No one is ever left idle, except upon reaching the age of 60, when men settle down to enjoy their well-earned rest. In summer time all work is suspended between hours of 11 to 3 in the afternoon. All work stops at noon on Saturdays.

"The tilling of the land is all done in one piece. There are no hedges nor divisions of the whole 2900 acres as far as ownership is concerned. Men are put to work at whatever task they are best suited for, and may be changed to another, more congenial to them, if it means greater efficiency. Some are at work in the fields, while others are engaged in machine shops, others in gardening, etc. Laziness is very seldom met.

"A writer in the Victoria Daily Times says: 'It is the socialist Utopia, the realization of equality which is being advocated for the rest of the world to-day.'

"There are no cares as to where the next day's meals are to come from. There is no stinting or grudging to provide sustenance when one's strength has ebbed in declining years. There are no divisions between 'mine' and 'thine'; no man is richer than his fellow; therefore there are no jealousies or envy as to the possessions of another.

"Cares as to money are totally absent. One member of the executive does all the outside buying and selling. Any money received by individual members from outside sources is turned into the treasury. It would have no purchasing value within the community, nor is there any need for it, for food and clothing and all necessaries of life are doled out from the various departments in charge of these matters.

"The government is in the hands of the people, effectively and simply, altho without any machinery of government whatever. Once a week all persons, both men and women, who have reached years of mature understanding crowd into the large assembly house, which has a capacity of 2000, and discuss the affairs of the community. At these meetings, held every Sunday afternoon, the manager of each department is given his instructions according to the popular sentiment. No definite time is specified at the appointment of an officer, but he holds office as long as he does his work well. This is the initiative, referendum and recall system without the cumbersome machinery in use at the present day.

"All the houses are built pretty much after the same plan. Like everything built or used or worn by the Doukhobours, their residences are devoid of all elaborateness or ornamentation of any kind, but eminently substantial and practical for all intents and purposes. They are built in pairs, and at a respectful distance from other buildings for sanitary reasons and fire isolation. There is an abundance of air and light. Each dwelling accommodates no less than thirty people. Married folks have double bedrooms. All beds are taken out of doors every morning and given a thorough sunning and airing. At the rear of each pair of buildings there is a bath house, with a boiler in the center, supplying steam for the hot room and hot water for the numerous baths around.

"All the women of each household take turns at cooking and baking the bread for all the inmates. The food is very appetizing and well cooked. Needless to say, the Doukhobours eat no meat or eggs. The first impression which strikes a stranger entering a Doukhobour settlement at night is the absolute stillness of the place, which at first seems almost uncanny. One realizes before long that this is due to the absence of either dogs or poultry in the place. The Doukhobours have no use for either, since chickens cannot be raised or sold for any other purpose than eating, and dogs would have nothing to watch.

"The men look hale and sturdy and the children are almost without exception pictures of blossoming health. * * * All have an inquiring, inquisitive look, for strangers are not seen every day; yet disrespect is totally absent * * * The top floor of the great assembly house contains several big class rooms.

"They have a large and well-appointed hospital at Brilliant, and they have everything there except doctors, nurses, or inmates. The building is inhabited by a superannuated and very affable janitor. Each dwelling comprises two special emergency rooms—one of them adapted for women in confinement.

"The Doukhobours show great consideration and solicitude for their women. As a general rule, no family is incumbered with more than two or three children. Equality of sexes has reached its highest expression in their social life. Women are recognized as being competent to judge upon all of the affairs of their community. Not only do they share in all administrative work and take part in all the councils, but they also perform all the religious rites and conduct divine services on the same footing with men. Prayers are always held in the open, weather permitting. The congregation always stands, not only bareheaded, but barefooted as well, in summer. Prayer books they have none, neither is there a place of worship in the direct sense. They have no written laws or rules and no written prayers. There is nothing fixed or moulded in their worship—it is a live and spontaneous religion.

"The figure of Peter Verigin, the leader of the entire Doukhobour sect now in America, is one of almost awe-inspiring personality. He is the seventh leader of the Doukhobour sect, which has been in existence for 200 years. Preceding him was a woman, Lookeria Vassilevna. She found and marked Verigin for leadership when he was a mere boy. He belonged to a very wealthy family of the Doukhobour persuasion and he followed her implicitly. He was given a thorough education and prepared very painstakingly to assume this important post, which she passed on to him on her deathbed. No sooner had he assumed the leadership than he started a movement of passive resistance to the Russian government's system of compulsory military service. He was soon seized by the authorities and exiled to Siberia. He was kept in exile for sixteen years—long after the last of the Doukhobours migrated from Russia. But he never relinquished leadership.

"He maintained a constant correspondence with Count Leo Tolstoy, who was an ardent champion of the Doukhobours' cause. Tolstoy never sold the copyright for his books or accepted any royalties from the publishers, but he made exception in the case of the novel 'Resurrection,' the proceeds of which went to assist the Doukhobours in migrating from Russia. Peter Verigin is now 55 years old. He is possessed of a powerful constitution and a quiet energy which knows no obstacles and no defeat. Yet he is simple, affable, and good natured in the extreme. He is constantly oscillating among all of the Doukhobour settlements attending to all matters accumulating during his absence."

* * * * *

The persecutions of the Doukhobours were by no means over when they emigrated to Canada. They came into conflict with minor officials, first in the matter of land patents in Saskatchewan, and later in Alberta. They claim that more than 40 men and women were put in prison at Regina for three months. They were beaten and tormented for refusing to eat meat, and given the most humiliating tasks. They were forcibly given medicine and food, being burned with scalding soup during the feeding. They claim that seven were mistreated so that death followed as a result. The causes of these tortures were not infractions of laws, they claim, but because the prisoners would not eat meat. Their refusal to give statistics regarding birth and deaths has led to reprisals by officials in British Columbia.

In an article written for Farm and Home of Vancouver, B. C. (in September, 1922., Mr. J. S. Dunn says: "I had a demonstration of the repugnance the Doukhobours have for killing anything. I saw a bunch of tent caterpillars sunning themselves on a large limb of an apple tree, and called to two of the youths with me to get something to kill them; the boys looked but would not act, so I went after the nasty pests and made short work of them. The boys could not look upon the massacre and turned away in mute but horrified protest. * * *

"The Doukhobours are very hospitable to strangers and do not accept payment for any entertainment they furnish to such. * * *

"After passing over the block and examining the growing crops, I have no hesitation in saying it is the best-cultivated big block of land I have ever seen in British Columbia. The Doukhobours, men and women alike, seem to be natural gardeners * * * The plan their season's work well ahead and are careful not to undertake more than they can accomplish comfortably; they figure on having a fair surplus of labor for their undertaking. They are forehanded in the things they buy, and purchase in car lots wherever possible from wholesalers or manufacturers * * *.

"A material factor that forms a strong bond for holding the Doukhobours together is the fact that while members of the community they have no fear of adversity. They are always assured of a comfortable home, food, and clothing as long as they live. * * * One commendable rule of the community is that when the age of sixty is reached all work stops for the individual at his option; but he retains his home and gets his food and clothing just as he did when working, and he gets it as his right and not as a matter of charity. He has earned it."

Mr. Dunn believes that much of the success is due to the strong and capable management of Peter Verigin, who goes from community to community, everywhere being received with esteem and love by his people. Harry Bell, a resident of the Llano Colony in Louisiana, who has been among the Doukhobours, says that Verigin is usually followed by several attendents, and travels in good class, dresses well, and fully understands the value of making a good personal impression. His contacts with business associates outside the colony or firms with which he transacts business does not subject him to any inferiority-complex.

"The principal settlements," resumes Mr. Dunn, "in B. C. are Brilliant, Grand Forks, Pass Creek, Glade, and Shoreacres, where the Community owns and pays taxes on 20,664 acres. * * *

"As Verigin gets off the train, he is at once surrounded by a joyous crowd of singing men, women, and children * * * who shower him with flowers if flowers are to be had. * * *

"Verigin has, however, some critics among his own people, and when occasion offers, these are by no means backward in voicing their opinions. A few of the Doukhobours have broken with the community and have gone ranching on their own account. I found several of these in the neighborhood of Thrums * * * Some keep stock and poultry and a few eat fish and meat and are little by little falling into the habits of the Anglo-Saxons. It is difficult, however, to induce the women to break with the community, for they observe that the lives of their sisters who have become independent are harder and their living is not so comfortable as that provided by the community. * *

"The general office building is spacious and modern (at Brilliant), the offices being furnished with plain flat-topped desks, desk telephones, filing cabinets, typewriters, etc., as are also the offices in the different department buildings and system prevails over all. Systematic co-operation is the cornerstone upon which has been built the great agricultural success of the Doukhobours. I had lunch in the great dining room provided for the workers in the warehouses, and the meal—strictly vegetarian—could not have been more appetizing or satisfying. The bowl of vegetable soup handed me by a barefooted waitress was a revelation in the culinary art. * * * "

"We started on a tour of inspection. The land along the north side of the river is rocky and broken, making it difficult and expensive for road-building. My attention was called to the quality of the road we were traveling over. It was excellent, smooth and wide, with easy grades, though much of it was cut out of the solid rock, and every bit of it built at the expense of the community alone. I traveled over miles and miles of these roads which have all been made by the Doukhobours with not a dollar of assistance from the government. Yet the general public finds these roads of great utility. * * * And bear in mind, the community did not get these lands for nothing; they bought them, paying from $50 to $500 an acre. * * *

"To reach he community's largest tract of cultivated land, we had to cross to the south side of the Kootenay river, which we did over a fine suspension steel bridge. This bridge, which is used by the general public, was erected by the Doukhobours at a cost of $50,000, the government assisting to the extent of $20,000 Just across the bridge to the west is the great irrigation pump—said to be the most powerful one in the country for this purpose—which lifts the water needed by many hundreds of acres * * * The sight resented by this extensively cultivated block of 2000 acres, without a fence or an animal in sight except the work stock, is certainly unique * * * Possibly 90 per cent of this great block of land is growing fruits and vegetables. * * *

"The irrigation project is one of considerable magnitude. The plans are made by a member of the society who is a civil engineer whom we found at the dam dressed in overalls just like the rest of the workers and superintending the job. More than half of the job was done when I viewed it, and rapid progress was being made with the remainder by the sixty men the engineer had on the job. The irrigation system entails an expenditure of about $100,000 in cash, which the community is bearing alone. This does not take into account the labor expended on the undertaking, as the work has been done by the members of the community in the ordinary way. The money comes from the profits the society has made and goes to prove the statement that when they make profits the money is used in improving their holdings. * *

"When I visited their jam factory, I found an up-to-date plant in every respect. Everything was clean and bright as a new linen table cloth. The manager took me thru and was painstaking in explaining the workings. They were hard at work on gooseberries, which are always taken from the pickers and delivered at the factory the day they are picked. This rule is carried out in the handling of all other fruits during the season and is the secret—together with the rule to pack nothing but the best—of the great demand for their products.

"This year they will have an output of about 60 carloads of jam, contracts having been made already for about 45 cars and fresh orders coming footed waitress was a revelation in the culinery art. * * *"
year have doubled and trebled their orders. * * *"

* * * * *

The history of the Doukhobours is the history of a people who offer passive resistance, but who are not to be swerved from that they think is right. They have practiced the same principles that the followers of Gandhi are using in India. They offer no resistance to violence and do not resort to violence, yet they do not submit passively to wrongs. They are willing to make any sacrifices which may become necessary. They remain true to their principles in spite of all.

It is not astonishing that they have been singularly successful in their colonization. Their communal life is peaceful and largely unperturbed by the things which cause misery and unhappiness in the outer world. Holding the beliefs they do, and animated by the principles which guide them, they are particularly well equipped for communal life. It might be said that no people not holding principles of this kind can be so equipped, and one of the most common causes of failure of secular colonies is the lack of these principles of love and toleration and consideration of the rights and opinions of others.

Those who do not accept the Bible and who have the utmost scorn for religious forms and ceremonies and practices, can learn much from these simple people. They have the essence of Christianity, stripped of most of its form. Many will not agree with all they do or believe; yet the Doukhobours have sound fundamental principles which have been amply tested, far more amply tested than the theories of which many more militant reformers are so enamored. The Doukhobours have used love as a principle, and they practice it. Those who scorn love as a practical principle or recipe for success might well hesitate and make some comparisons. It might be salutary to place in comparison some of the secular organizations which have permitted intolerance, hatred, and militancy to become a part of the fabric of their motives, and measure them with the simple directness and universal love which is the central thought of the successful Doukhobours.

HOUSE OF DAVID

1903 to Present Time

The House of David at Benton Harbor, Michigan, is another of those religious colonies with strong leaders and based on the second coming of Christ. Several letters written to the House of David brought tardy and brief answers, a letter signed "E. M." reading:

"Ernest S. Wooster,

Dear Sir:—Since writing you we have been so busy with our work there that we have not had time to settle down on any articles. We are still engaged in court cases, so we hardly know where to begin writing until we get settled again * * *"

Court cases were instituted in 1923 against Benjamin, head of the House of David were made much of by the press and dragged through the courts for many months. However, at a later date, in answer to specific questions, it was possible to get some definite information regarding the House of David.

This religious association is based on the belief that 144,000 of the children of Israel are to be gathered together, and preparations are being made for them at Benton Harbor. In this respect the belief is much the same as that of the people of the Koreshan Unity at Estero, Florida, who are also making preparations for an ingathering of 144,000 people. The Koreshans had as their leaders Koresh (Cyrus Teed) and Victoria Gratia, his dual associate. The latter was expected to become the mother of the 144,000 sons of God. The leaders of the House of David are Benjamin and Mary, and they have been rather more successful in the gathering of members, as they have, according to information from the House of David given by letter to the author in August, 1924, about 1000 members.

The beliefs of the House of David adherents are that the 144,000 of the elect are to be gathered at Benton Harbor, and that they will become free from the power of death, they and their posterity to reign over the people of the earth. They prophesied some years prior to the war that great tribulation would come upon all that did not accept the offer of salvation and immorality, and that the 144,000 (288,000 with the women) would pass to England, thence to Palestine, where the final Kingdom of God would be established according to the Scriptures. The prophecy made was: "The Valley of Jehosophat will open wide her jaws and the blood of the slain and wounded will flow in the valleys; for great and terrible will be the day of the Lord, which is now fast approaching. The world may cry: Peace! peace! but there will be no peace, but war! war! with all of its miseries, pestilences, famines, and diseases — nor will it be confined to Europe alone, but the whole planet will be one scene of bloodshed * * * " This prophecy was made many years ago and was expected to take place before 1916.

Benjamin Purnell, and Mary, are not the first of the House of David, but the seventh of its prophets, the dates going back to 1792. The honest and sincere members of the House of David do not use liquor or tobacco, nor eat meat. They are celibates. They wear their hair long and do this on the command of Christ, "Ye shall not round the corners of your heads, neither shalt thou mar the corners of thy beard."

Altho the writer has come in only small contact with the members of this remarkable organization, and speaks from the meager knowledge of knowing but one family of them, he is convinced that their religion has a tremendous hold on them. Ridicule is not effective in breaking their faith. The colony at Benton Harbor, however, does not accept all of its adherents who apply to become community residents, but uses some sort of system of testing the fitness of members, evidently, as the family alluded to was refused admittance on the grounds of "not having the right conditions." This apparently referred to not having the right spiritual or psychological attitude, for others without means have been accepted.

According to the information gleaned from the questionaire sent to the House of David, there is a branch in Australia, though the importance of this is not stated. The number of persons at Benton Harbor is given at "some less than one thousand." They reply concerning the number of acres under cultivation with "several tracts of farm land, ranging from 20 acres to four hundred in each tract, not all valuable," so we may infer that their holdings are at least upwards of one thousand acres. The chief crops are fruits, berries, hay, and grain. The industries operated are machine shops, printing shop, dairy, a summer resort at Eden Springs, hotel and restaurant, aviary and zoo, greenhouse, miniature railway, and an income is derived from the hotel and park, band, baseball team, sale of souvenirs.

The House of David has no school system of its own, sending its children to the public schools. Perhaps a lack of interest in education of children may grow out of the idea of celibacy, which naturally has no place for children in it.

The social life consists of baseball, band, orchestra, mandolin club, dialogues, plays. The traveling baseball teams and band have become widely known thruout the country.

No money value has been placed on the properties. The members have their needs supplied and are contented. The chief feature of the organization was given as "Life teaching, or the redemption of the body without death, and without the body going to the grave. This is a profound teaching, and in order to understand it, one should get our literature and study for himself or herself, and not go by report or hearsay."

Asked as to the number of adherents outside the Colony, the writer was referred to the literature. The organization is described as being "An apostolic commonwealth wherein all labor for the common good." No particular method of ridding the community of the discontented is followed, apparently. Perhaps there have not been many of them in this apparently very successful community.

LLANO CO-OPERATIVE COLONY
1914 to Present Time

The Llano Co-operative Colony, incorporated as the Llano del Rio Company of Nevada, now located at Newllano, Vernon Parish, Louisiana, is one of the secular colonies which has been able to survive long enough to establish certain definite principles and traditions which seen to point the way to permanency. Like many other secular colonies, it suffered from the conflicts which grow out of purely materialistic reasons for entering a community, reasons which have been amply demonstrated as being the causes of failure. It was thru a change in psychology, the establishment of new ethical understandings, an awakening and chrystalized idealism, in which the founder, Job Harriman, took the lead, as he did in many other things, that established the more highly ethical or spiritual conditions which seem to provide the foundation necessary for success without making it a religious basis. The use of the word "spiritual" here is not to be confused with the meaning given by religious people.

Job Harriman, at the time he founded the Llano Colony, was a leading criminal lawyer of Los Angeles, attaining national prominence in this field as he became associated with the defense in the McNamara dynamiting cases in Los Angeles when the Los Angeles Times building was dynamited. At the same time he was candidate for mayor of the city on a joint Labor and Socialist ticket with every prospect of success, and had previously been candidate for governor on the Socialist ticket. He was at one time candidate for vice-president on the same ticket with Eugene V. Debs. During a score of years of activity in the labor and Socialist organizations he became well known to radicals throughout the country because of his clear thinking and his ability to accurately forecast coming events. He was never a professional agitator, nor did he make the radical movement a means of livelihood. He gave of his time and talents freely.

In notes on Llano Colony dictated in 1924 to be used in a forthcoming history of Llano Colony, Mr. Harriman made clear the reasons which caused him to launch the Llano Colony. Early failure of the enterprise was prophesied by his many friends.

"In 1900 or about that time, I became convinced that the Socialist party as a political organization was not functioning as it should. It seemed to me that the organization should be essentially a propaganda movement with political activities in such places only as there were no labor political activities, and that we should never put a ticket in the field in opposition to a labor ticket, regardless of the platform of the labor party. The reason for this attitude was the same as the reason I felt in regard to what our attitude should be toward the labor organizations. It seemed to me that the economic organization of the working class determined the political policy of the entire class just as the economic power of our capitalist class determined the political policy of that class.

"It seemed to me, and I advocated it, that we should not permit any one to join the Socialist party unless he first became a member of some trade union * * * and that our propaganda in the trade-union movement should be conducted on personal lines and not in the unions during hours of business; that our members should state their position frankly and openly in regard to strikes and labor troubles, and, if the decision of the movement were against them, that it was our duty to support the strike the same as we would have supported it had we favored it, and that it should be incumbent on our members to do whatever strike or picket duty might be assigned to them, and in every way to act to their best ability to the end that the strike might be a success, suffering the loss of position or imprisonment or whatever befell those in the struggle.

"* * * I held this position and frequently argued it with those prominent in the Socialist Party, but with no avail until the metal workers' strike arose in 1910 on the Pacific Coast. During that strike the Los Angeles Socialist local was induced to move to the Labor Temple and to lend every support to the union men on strike. Out of the combination there arose a joint political movement. The Socialist Party organized branches all over the city and county of Los Angeles, with a strong central committee. The Labor Unions organized a Union Labor Political Club to which they sent delegates from practically all the unions. From the Union Labor Political Club delegates were sent to the County Central Committee of the Socialist Party. This was contrary to the constitution of the Socialist Party, but there was no other way of which we knew by which the unions could be represented in the county committee, and for this reason the Constitution was violated.

"A joint campaign was conducted on the enthusiasm that was aroused by reason of the strike and by reason of the arrest of the McNamaras, whom the labor movement in Los Angeles thought innocent. This created great enthusiasm, and the Socialist and Labor ticket would have been elected by a large majority had the McNamaras not pleaded guilty five days before election.

"Some time after this campaign, the Socialists who were more or less opposed to the combination raised the constitutional objection with the National Committee. * * * It resulted in a complete separation of the two movements and the collapse of the Socialist Party in Los Angeles.

"I was so impressed with the fact that the movement must have an economic foundation that I turned my attention to the study of means by which we could lay some such foundation, even tho it be a small one as well as an experimental one. After two or three years, I decided to try to establish a co-operative colony. This was undertaken in Los Angeles County, California, at the mouth of the Big Rock Creek, about 45 miles from Los Angeles, due north, or about 90 miles by road.

"To accomplish this purpose, I proposed to organize a joint stock company in which each member should purchase two thousand shares, paying for 1000 in cash or property, and paying for the other 1000 shares by labor. The reason for this was to give each an equal voting power. * * We provided that each member of the colony who was engaged in work for the colony, either at the colony or at some other place, should receive $4 a day. It was understood that those working in the colony should equally receive only as much as was necessary to feed and clothe them and one dollar a day as payment on their stock until their other thousand shares should be paid for, and the balance was to accumulate as credit until the net returns from the colony should be sufficient to pay them.

"This would lay an economic foundation, as. it seemed, of equal ownership and pay. We established at the first a social system which was free alike to all, with no charges for amusement, whether it was dancing, moving pictures, or what not. The reason for this position was that high-class entertainments could be furnished if no charges were made, whereas if charges were made, many would demand things to which they had been accustomed, and thus prevent the social uplift which we imagined would follow in the trail of refined entertainments.

"These three elements, then—equal ownership, equal wage, and equal social opportunities—were the fundamental principles of the colony. * * * With these points in view I gathered eight men besides myself."

The first move was to buy the Mescal Land & Water Company, which was at Mescal Creek and was capitalized at $50,000. This was to get into action quickly, as another company was buying land at the mouth of Big Rock. The purchase of property in both places began, and $5 was the first actual sum paid, upon which the Llano Colony was founded; it was given as earnest money on a $80,000 deal! Later the Llano del Rio Company was organized with a capitalization of $2,000,000. Mr. Harriman had the theory of the colony will in mind, having been working on it for many years, and it was accepted without question. He says:

"Having been a Socialist for 23 years and a believer in the theory of economic determinism, and in Marx' philosophy of surplus value as determined by the social labor power necessary to produce products, and the belief in materialistic conception of life, I assumed that if a co-operative colony could be established in which an environment were created that would afford each individual an equal and social advantage, that they would, in a comparatively short time, react harmoniously to this environment and the extreme selfishness and greed as it appears in the capitalist and in men of conflicting interests would be done away. It was my theory that this would be especially true if we could establish a school that would grow into a colony institution, finally engulfing all of the members of the colony in mingled educational and industrial pursuits. I was confident that the scientific knowledge would increase the efficiency in the industrial field sufficiently to allure all into the school, and that the mental development, along with the economic advantage, would work out such a degree of harmony as is necessary to the permanency of community life.

I also thot that the social relations as stated above were vital, and that every uplifting social means within our reach should be adopted as the refining influence necessary to the intellectual, cultural, and economic condition of the colony. The purpose of all this was to show that a community could live together in harmony, could produce its own living, direct all of its members, maintain a higher standard of living than is usually maintained—and all with far less labor.

"I thought that if this could be done then we could use this community as an example by which other communities could be built. I realized, in a way, that the economic condition was vital, and, while I thot it was the determining factor, I still felt that a study of the mind in the most scientific way was likewise necessary, although I at that time hinged practically everything on the materialistic theory and the theory of economic determinism.

The purpose, in addition to the establishing of other colonies, was to build an institution or a colony that would have vision and a value beyond the mere welfare of the individuals in the colony, and would become a matter of large social interest, teaching the possibilities of community life."

Big Rock Creek, where the start was made, showed about 20,000 inches of water when it was investigated, but subsequent experience showed that it did not maintain this splendid flow. A development company had a few years previously organized and bonded a district, pushed a tunnel through a hill parallel to the creek, and exhausted its funds so that it had to quit work, and its settlers moved away. There was seemingly a good location with a valuable tunnel to conduct the water part of the distance. It was several years before the serious flaw in the whole thing was discovered; this was an earthquake fault which took up much of the water in years of small precipitation. The reservoir sites, which seemed adequate for a far larger storage capacity than the colony would need, were found to be deceiving, and were far less than their apparent size.

The soil was a disintegrated granite, splendid for pears and other fruit trees, and for alfalfa. It would grow melons and some other crops the first year; but it was so deficient in humus that there was not the productivity that was imperative. The chemist who examined the soil failed to take into consideration the mechanical properties; the bottomless coarse sand did not hold humus or fertilizer well.

The location was almost ideal. Situated on a broad, pleasant mesa, it commanded a view of the great Antelope Valley, offshoot of the Mojave Desert, and in the clear air hills fifteen miles appeared to be but five, while it was possible to see the smoke of trains forty or fifty miles away. The mountains to the south were covered with snow until June, and the peaks sometimes into August. There were majestic pine forests, a small lake, strange rock formations, springs, creeks, and many alluringly beautiful spots.

The method of financing was the sale of stock, but this was not done in the usual capitalistic or promotive manner. Before stock was sold, the prospective member was required to file a formal application for membership, and this application was acted on by the Board of Directors. The original plan was to require $500 cash, but this was raised by degrees until within 18 months the rate was $1000 as originally intended for initial payments. Each person entered into a contract to purchase a total of 2000 shares, constituting a full membership, a portion of which was paid in cash at the time of entering, the remainder to be worked out at the rate of $1 a day. This contract also stipulated employment of the member at the rate of $4 for eight hours' work, one dollar to apply on membership, the remaining $3 to be used for living expenses and to accumulate as credits to be paid eventually in cash from the sale of products. This arrangement was changed after about four years.

In order to expedite matters, one C. V. Eggleston was employed as fiscal agent to sell stock. His methods were soon discontinued, however, and he was discharged within a few months. At this time the Blue Sky Law went into operation and the Llano del Rio Company was refused the right to sell stock. The statement of conditions upon which this decision was based was made by an agent sent by the Commissioner of Corporations to investigate the colony. The statement contained some truths, many false assertions, and many unwarranted deductions.

Meanwhile, Eggleston had gone to Nevada and organized the Nevada Colony Company for the purpose of launching a colony enterprise of his own. When the privilege of selling stock was withdrawn, the Llano Colony made arrangements with Eggleston whereby his corporation purchased all of the California property, stock in his company being taken in exchange. By this device it became possible to sell stock in the new company, soon to be renamed the Llano del Rio Company of Nevada, in California. The

Llano Colony was the first of 5000 corporations which did the same thing, or pursued some similar plan. The Commissioner threatened Mr. Harriman and the Board of Directors with criminal proceedings, but Mr. Harriman explained to the Commissioner that the stock had been purchased in a regular business way and was already issued and that it was therefore out of his jurisdiction. He did not prosecute. In a test case later with another company, Mr. Harriman's point was upheld.

However, the deal with Eggleston, who later was connected with the colony at Fallon, was completed only by watching that gentleman with utmost care. A shrewd insight into his methods saved the colony from being delivered into his hands, but not until he thought this had been done and he had given expression to a premature boast of triumph.

The Llano Colony grew rapidly despite unfavorable publicity and the coldness, amounting to suspicion, showed by the Socialists and other radicals. This was due in a very large degree to the fact that Mr. Harriman was very well known, especially thruout the West, and the Socialists held him in high repute. The rapid growth brought a train of problems. Housing and transportation were foremost among these, though from the first the lack of finances was a serious source of worry. Most of the people were sheltered in tents, later some in thin-walled adobe houses, and a few in frame houses. A substantial and really artistic hotel was built, though later somewhat marred by an unsightly rough addition. Two ample adobe industrial buildings were put up, one housing the laundry, cannery, baths, and printing plant, the other housing the shoeshop and woodworking industries. A frame building adjoining it sheltered other industries and the warehouse.

A fine dairy barn with a cement-laid boulder base, a dairy house, and a concrete silo were built. The rock work was laid for a large horse barn. One of the biggest rabbitries in the United States was constructed and housed 3000 rabbits at one time. There was a modern poultry house, an office with stone vault, and a dormitory of about 24 rooms. Rock-lined ditches were built, the rock being laid in mortar made from lime burned by colonists.

The orchard contained about 140 acres of pears and 80 acres of apples near the colony townsite and about 80 acres near Mescal, tho the latter did not do well. There were 240 acres of alfalfa. The dairy had about 100 cows, good stock. There was a range herd of about as many. The thirty registered Duroc sows and two boars, occupied a modern and well-built hog barn. The cannery in 1917 put out two carloads of tomatoes, one of which was shipped to Louisiana when the move was made to that place. There were apples and pears and other fruits and vegetables as well, and some experiments had been made in canning rabbits. Fruit was obtained not from the colony orchards, but by sending out groups of colonists to nearby orchards where they worked, their wages being paid to the colony in fruit. The printing department put out a monthly and a weekly publication. The bakery supplied the colony with bread; cider and vinegar were made as an adjunct to the cannery work. The shoeshop repaired shoes for colonists. There was a tinshop, a cabinet shop, a sawmill, and much wood-working machinery. The colony band at one time contained thirty pieces, and there were nearly 700 persons in the colony at about the time it was decided that a new location must be sought.

The schools consisted of a grammar school under state regulations, and independent industrial school in charge of George T. Pickett; the latter employed the children during a portion of each day. The Montessori school was the largest in the state. No high school had been firmly established, though several attempts were made to do this. The colony took a contract to build a grammar school, and this was finished just as the move was made from California to Louisiana.

One of the institutions at Llano, California, was the General Assembly, which was organized early in the history of the colony. It did not have any particular rights, but as the expression of public opinion, of course, it had all of the rights which could have been delegated to it in any formal way. This body continued during the entire time the colony was located in California. Co-existent with it for a few months was the Commission, with duties clearly enough defined, but with no real authority and much in conflict with the General Assembly. There was at all times the official and legally-responsible Board of Directors, and there grew up as a sort of colony executive committee the Board of Managers, constituted of heads of departments. These men met every evening, reported on their day's work, and laid plans for the coming day. It was quite efficient in its operations, and was in marked contrast to the General Assembly, as it substituted industrial for political management.

As is the history of other communities, the General Assembly was a place where personal grievances were frequently aired, where colony politicians and chronic trouble-makers had a splendid opportunity to keep things in turmoil, and where the general uneasiness which is likely to attend such enterprise as the colony was increased rather than abated. Much of the discussion was acrimonious; personal vindictiveness and bitterness caused many foremen to be singled out for attack; and the whims and irresponsibility of the Assembly made it a most serious obstacle in the path of progress and order.

Although the General Assembly seemed an expression of Democracy, the lack of personal responsibility on the part of members, and the frequent lack of knowledge of the subjects discussed made it rather a hotbed of politics, vindictiveness, rivalries, suspicion, and discord, rather than a democratic assembly. The democracy of it was more apparent than real, for the inflamed passions and the excited utterances, together with the tenseness of the general atmosphere, made any dispassionate or calm consideration of problems almost impossible. When this is coupled with the fact that many of the people were positive in their opinions and strong in their convictions, quarrelsome and argumentative, it is easy to understand that the General Assembly, at least as conducted there, was open to serious criticism. Most of the minds were receptive to suspicion, and there was suspicion sowed at every opportunity. If democracy means consideration of facts with a previous knowledge of the conditions and a general knowledge of the subject, then the General Assembly was not democratic, for it required of its members traits and information which only a small minority possessed. Any vote taken by such a body would be a vote of the passions and opinions of the moment. This is shown by the frequency with which the Assembly reversed its own decisions and changed its plans.

The colony made good progress despite this chaotic government, its newness, its disadvantageous location, its lack of funds, and the mistake of founding it on purely materialistic philosophy. It accumulated much property. Had the water supply been what it seemed, there would have been no doubt of the opportunity before it. But a careful investigation disclosed the fact that the water was inadequate, and it was upon this discovery that the decision was made to find another location.

Some idea of the development can be gained from the list of industries, institutions, and organizations which was printed in 1917 in the official literature, and which shows that much progress had been made. These were:

Print shop, shoe shop, laundry, cannery, cleaning, warehouse, machine shop, blacksmith shop, rug works, planing mill, range stock, hog-raising, dairy goats, soap-making, lumbering, magazine, newspaper, bakery, fish hatchery, transportation, barber shop, overall and shirt shop, paint shop lime kiln, saw mill, dairy, cabinet shop, nursery, alfalfa, orchards, poultry yards, gardens, rabbitry.

This literature also carried this paragraph:

In addition to the industries are many institutions that are almost industries and which might be classed as such. There are also the recreations which deserve special mention.

Baths, swimming pool, studio, two hotels, drafting room, post office, commissary, camping grounds, industrial school, grammar school, Montessori school, commercial classes, fishing and hunting, library, two weekly dances, night classes, brass band, mandolin club, orchestras, quartets, baseball, football and basketball, Socialist local, entertainments.

The property in Louisiana was directed to Mr. Harriman's attention by a member who came from Texas. A trip of investigation was made by a committee appointed by the assembled colonists, and on its return a report was presented to the colonists. After a careful consideration of the matter, the vote was unanimous to establish a colony in Louisiana. This, however, did not mean abandonment of the California property. It was thought, and many still hold, that the California property would support a small population and could be brought to productiveness and made very profitable. There seemed to be no obstacle to this, and a number of efficient men were retained there. W. A. Engle was left in charge of the ranch, but Gentry P. McCorkle was in general charge, especially of the financial affairs.

By the sale of much of the chattel property, and by borrowing money from members, the colonists, those who wished to change, were taken to Louisiana in December, 1917. A few had preceded the special train in automobiles, and a half dozen or so had come on ahead by train. Many of the colonists did not want to go to Louisiana, and left the colony to go out for themselves. Probably a majority of these expected soon to rejoin the colony.

Meanwhile, the man who had directed attention to the Louisiana property, a tract of 20,000 acres at Stables, near Leesville, Louisiana, had been active, and, true to his promise, had brought about twenty-five families from northeast Texas. Many of these were unable to read and write, and their understanding of integral co-operation as applied in the Llano Colony was doubtless very vague. What arguments were used to urge them to become members, it is difficult to state. It seems improbable that they could have had a very clear understanding of the ideals and purposes of the colony, and it was very soon apparent that their code of ethics was not quite in accord with the code which the more seasoned colonists had adopted. This became glaringly evident when an appraisal committee, made up of these people, valued the property turned in by them at sums greatly in excess of what it could be sold for. In one instance a stallion was turned in at $1,000 and was subsequently sold when returned to its owner, at less than $100. A sawmill of so little value that it was almost useless was given a high valuation; the boiler which was a part of it was eventually abandoned as not being worth moving when it was returned to its owner.

The Californians and the Texans did not get along well. The ideals were not the same, the methods were at wide variance, and friction soon grew up. The man who had brought them in, together with two others, headed an insurrection. It was believed that a pool of oil is under the property, and a bold attempt was made by the promoter to seize possession. The effort was not successful, but it left the colony weak and stripped of property. The Texans nearly all departed, taking with them as a result of a compromise settlement, a large majority of all of the implements and livestock which it was expected to use in putting in the crop. The first payment on the land had not yet been made, and this was made the object of suspicion. The Texans refused to work, and made many threats, some including the life of Mr. Harriman, and of the writer. These threats were quite serious, though only one or two actual attempts at violence were made. There was a period when each day brought its daily threat.

Just before this, Mr. Harriman had been recalled to California, as an effort was being made there at the same time to seize that property. Here is Mr. Harriman's account of this, tho he made one or two trips to Louisiana during the efforts to straighten out the California affairs.

"When we left California, Mr. McCorkle was secretary, and as soon as I came down here, he began to plot against the interests of the colony to gain possession of all the property for himself. He caused the Tilghman place (most valuable of our possessions there) to be lost and purchased it in the name of his wife, and entered into contracts with adverse interests by which he became beneficiary in many instances concerning both land and water. Under threats of foreclosure of mortgage, he forced the leasing of the entire place to outside parties, and, by co-operating with them, he stripped the ranch of most of the valuable machinery and livestock. He then began foreclosure proceedings.

"Upon hearing of the foreclosure proceedings, I returned to California and told McCorkle that his transactions in the eyes of the law either in his name or that of his wife, were the transactions of a trustee, and that whatever he acquired either in his name or his wife's was held by them as trustees for the colony because he was a member of the colony and an officer of the Board when the same was acquired. His attorney evidently accepted this theory, and we came to a compromise agreement whereby the mortgage should be foreclosed into the Llano Investment Company of which we should hold half the stock and he half, we to have two directors and he to elect two, and these to agree upon a fifth.

"This agreement was carried out, the directors elected, and half of the stock transferred to us. We went into court, permitting the judgment to go against us in the foreclosure proceedings without putting up any defense. I returned to Louisiana pending the advertisement and was to return to California as soon as the foreclosure proceedings and the sale under the advertisement were made to the Llano Investment Company, when it was agreed we should put up the property for sale, either as a whole or in lots and pay the debts with the proceeds and divide the remainder.

"Instead of complying with the agreement and carrying it out, he represented to the Board of Directors of the Llano Investment Company that he did not have the money with which to do it, but would do it as soon as he could procure the money. All this time he was advertising is a country paper that was not seen by the Board of Directors. When the advertising was completed, the sale was made, and McCorkle bought the property and took judgment for $27,000. The Board wired me and I returned to California at once.

"The rule is, in equity cases, that when one has a day in court and fails to present his case, the case will not again be opened, regardless of who suffers. But there is also another rule, and that is that when a contract is not intended to be kept when made, the court will reopen the case at the request of the party suffering. I was confident that I could prove there was no intention of keeping the contract when it was made, and proceeded upon this theory and won.

"The debts amounted to $85,000. All but $10,000 were cancelled, the balance of $10,000 or $12,000 being secured by mortgages and notes on land at Newllano. In addition to settling the debts, I procured 1000 acres of land, free from encumbrance, in the Isle of Pines, estimated at that time to be worth $50,000. Land in the Isle of Pines can be bought as low as $15 an acre, but most of the land we secured is very rich loam of which there is not much on the island, and for that reason is valued at a much higher price—$50 an acre."

The debts which remained after the settlement totalled about $17,000, instead of the $12,000 estimated at the time Mr. Harriman wrote the statement, but some were of such a nature that perhaps the lower figure will become the nearer one. The noteworthy achievement of reducing them from $85,000 to the lower figure, and offsetting this by land in the Isle of Pines, was not accomplished without the most extraordinary exertions. Mr. Harriman pledged his own personal property in doing this, and some of it the colony was not able to redeem, so that the loss to him was great.

His sacrifice was not measured in terms of dollars and cents. At a most critical period of the Louisiana colony's affairs, he was kept away, being denied the pleasure of working with the enterprise for which he had sacrificed everything, and for which he had risked his reputation. Before he was free from the cares of closing up the western estate, his health was so impaired that he had to take a trip to Brazil, and was unable to live in Louisiana during the rainy seasons. It was the supreme sacrifice for the ideals embodied in the enterprise he had formed. Not all of those for whom he had risked so much appreciated fully what his services were. In winning the suit in California, he saved the Louisiana enterprise, for the judgment of $27,000 would have wiped out the colony before it got fairly started.

The unfaithfulness of this one man McCorkle brought the hopes of the California enterprise to an end. What would undoubtedly have developed into a substantial and valuable estate was made a failure because of the grasping shortsightedness of one who considered his own interests first and did not hesitate to use the most unscrupulous means to gain his ends.

Meanwhile, affairs in Louisiana became critical. The Texans stopped work, held meetings, became inflamed with anger under the careful coaching of their leaders, and demanded a return of their property. A telegram was despatched to Mr. Harriman, who came at once. To avoid detection in Leesville, a code was extemporized, so that the telegram read, "Much Southern brush found. Small farms wanted. Come at once." Mr. Harriman knew that the word "brush" stood for dissatisfaction, and that "southern" referred to the Texas members. "Small farms wanted" signified to him very accurately that these men demanded a division of property.

During the absence of Mr. Harriman, which was much of the time after May, 1918, and for two periods prior to that, the writer of this was acting manager. He was selected, not because of any particular fitness, but because of a more complete knowledge of the rather intricate affairs of the colony than was possessed by any other one person in Louisiana at that time. He was only temporary manager, though the time was extended until he occupied the position for more than two years continuously. It was a period of great uncertainty.

The Texans drew up a series of demands, and upon the return of Mr. Harriman these were presented in a rather dramatic manner. Many threats had been made against him, and a body-guard of loyal colonists was formed; but Mr. Harriman refused to recognize any danger and would accept no protection of this sort. Finally the affair was adjusted by giving the dissatisfied ones all of the property they had brought in, taking a note signed by one of their members, secured by the colony corporation stock which had been issued to them. How they divided the property returned to them was not made public. Some of the seceders had put in money. The leader who had been most active in working up the plot and who expected to form a pool to take over the property had put in nothing at all.

Prior to the return of Mr. Harriman, the dissenters had called a meeting to be held in the school house. The acting manager and the assistant secretary, E. E. Irwin, were asked to attend. They in turn requested that no colonists who were loyal to the colony be present, but all go about their usual duties. The reason for this request was that the situation was felt to be dangerous, and they did not want any more causes for friction than were absolutely unavoidable. Most of the colonists remained away.

The meeting was for the purpose of receiving a statement which would show the amounts paid into the colony by the persons who had joined in Louisiana. Out of their suspicion, the dissenters required that this show cash only. The acting manager came prepared with a statement which showed this, as it had been expected. He prefaced the reading of it by explaining that many had put in both cash and property, but this was received as an attempt at evasion.

When the list was read it was found that the three most active leaders had put in an aggregate sum in cash of fifteen cents—an average of a nickle each! To those who had brought in cash, this was a shock. They had been led into a revolt against their own homes and property and investment by men who had nothing to lose, apparently. In justice to Mr. Dean, it should be mentioned that he put in $1999.85 in property, and the fifteen cents represented cash to make it an even $2000 for two memberships for himself and his son. The other two men had not put in a cent.

No one disputed these facts, and the amazement of the seceders who had put such faith in their leaders, overcame their anger against the Colony to such an extent that when two men tried to lash the crowd into a murderous fury, no response could be aroused, tho the atmosphere was tense.

After the settlement was made, the Texans began to drift away; it was crop season and they must get to farming. Many of them were fine men, but they had been led astray by listening to slanderous statements instead of trying to get facts.

In the very midst of the excitement, a man from Idaho came to the colony, a very unassuming individual who scarcely made his presence known. When things were at their very blackest, this man came into the office and said he wanted to purchase a membership and also to loan the colony money. He made a loan of $6000, which eventually became the basis of a new contract with the Gulf Lumber Company, owners of the land. Fred Donaldson, the savior of the situation, proved himself a good member. His faith in integral co-operation was so strong that the dissension rife at the time did not deter him from his purpose of joining.

But the plot to seize the land did not stop here. Shortly after the compromise was made with the Texans which ultimately resulted in their leaving, despite many threats of staying to execute vengeance, and some personal attacks on members of the colony, the abstracts from the Gulf Company arrived and a demand was made for the first payment. Those from whom it was expected to receive the money for this first payment had been deterred from coming, so nothing could be expected from that source.

It was decided that Mr. Harriman, who was still present, should go to St. Louis and lay the entire case before the Gulf Lumber Company officials. But this intention was learned by colony enemies, who were allied with powerfully intrenched Leesville officials, as was learned subsequently, and Mr. Harriman was indicted on a fictitious charge of misrepresentation. He was required to appear in court on May 19, which was the day he had expected to meet the Gulf Lumber officials in St. Louis. His case was not called and it was a year before he could get the case before the court to have it dismissed. The whole thing was plainly framed for the express purpose of making it impossible for him to go to St. Louis, evidently in the hope that the colony would lose its option on the land thru default. A year later it was definitely learned that a group had raised the money to take over the contract, presumably to exploit stock sales in wildcatting for oil, just as the leader of the seceders had previously expressed a desire to do.

The writer had to go to St. Louis in Mr. Harriman's place and face the officials of the Gulf Lumber Company with such excuses as he could, and with the necessity of explaining why Mr. Harriman could not be present.

Despite the dark outlook, the president and board of directors of the lumber company listened to a recital of plain facts and consented to make a new contract at the suggestion of the colony representative—a contract which would be much more favorable to the colony than the original one. Upon this new contract $6000 was paid and a deed taken for 100 acres of land. Fred Donaldson's money, which had been carried in the writer's inside coat pocket for a month, was now used to give the colony its first foundation, though the first land purchased was far from the colony townsite.

Progress began to be made. Hope was renewed. A strip of four acres with about 15 houses was purchased. A contract had already been made with one Scoggins for 80 acres of land lying just west of the colony townsite. Eventually he tried to squirm out of this, and, after a lawsuit, a compromise was made at a price much in advance of the agreed one.

But the colony's troubles were not yet over. Wages were high and labor was in demand. The colony had many workers who were highly skilled mechanics, and the allurement of high wages on the outside was almost irresistible. Coupled with this was the failure of crops in 1919, preceded by a partial failure in 1918, so that there was great privation inside the colony, and great prosperity outside. Several industries were started which were profitable, but the difficulty of meeting the bills which had been incurred—old debts from California and current expenses—was depressing, and many left, so that some of the industries had to be closed. This was true of the bakery and of the butcher shop. Through lack of funds the store no longer operated as a store. The woodyard sold wood in Beaumont at $6 a cord, f.o.b. cars at the colony siding. The shoeshop was very profitable, and for a time virtually supported the colony. The poultry department had done well, but the 1919 purchase of baby chickens had been disappointing, due to delivering inferior chicks which did not thrive, and it became necessary to sell the entire business.

Blue indeed was the outlook during this period. But in 1919 George T. Pickett was sent to Illinois and aroused some interest which resulted in several members eventually. An elderly couple came from New York, putting $1700 into memberships and loaning $6000, so that the second land payment was made, though it was several months late. New members began to come as conditions on the outside became worse. The financial and business depression of 1920 and 1921 brought a great many, so that the land payments were made and investments made in machinery. The improvement was steady.

George T. Pickett became manager early in 1920 and continued in this position. With much energy, with a positiveness which was commanding, and with an optimism which nothing could daunt, he brought members and raised money, expanding the colony rapidly. There was much to be done in laying foundations, and this work was done. Buildings were put up and improvements made. Among the latter were several new buildings and an electric plant, so that the colony had electric lights and street lights, as well as power for its growing list of industries.

As a result of Mr. Pickett's energy, Frank P. and Kate Richards O'Hare were induced to come to Llano Colony early in 1923, bringing with them their publication, the American Vanguard, previously known to 250,000 readers as the National Rip Saw, suppressed during the war. It had recently been resuscitated, and its subscription list showed 20,000 names, which was about the limit that the equipment of the colony printery could handle.

At the same time, or within a few months, W. E. Zeuch, a young educator holding degrees in a number of universities, organized Commonwealth College and Academy and brought to the Llano Colony this institution of higher education. It was planned as a school for hand and brain workers, and its applicants must stand a preliminary test as to character and purpose, but a less rigorous test as to previous schooling. The adding of this school to the Llano Colony attracted widespread attention, and many who had hesitated about joining the colony were now anxious to become members that their children might enjoy the superior advantages which it was expected the school and social life of the colony would open to them. The Academy was a three-year course complete; the College started with only the junior work the first year, the higher work to be added a year at a time. The work was of a nature to appeal to studious young men and women, who were selected carefully, and from the first the applications were greatly in excess of the number which it was possible to accept. Commonwealth was established as a common-law trust separate from the colony, but working in such close harmony with it as to be virtually an integral part, and depending for its economic base upon the colony. Special classes in the evening permitted adults to take up certain subjects, also.

Thus the Llano Co-operative Colony in 1924 had the following industries, institutions, and activities:

Brickyard, harness shop, theater, swimming pool, dances, orchestras, dormitories for boys and girls, wagon-making, crate-making, blacksmith shop, machine shop, garage, bakery, printshop, book bindery, hotel, store, commissary, hospital, peanut-butter-making, sawmill, broom-making, steam laundry, shoe shop, library, cannery, shingle mill. kindergarten, grammar school, Academy and High school, College.

Under the head of Agriculture was listed the following:

Two dairies, milk goat herd, Angora goats, sheep, poultry, gardening, orchards, rice-growing, miscellaneous crops

Some of these were only partly commercial, and some were purely service departments intended to lighten the work or to add to the pleasure of living in the colony. Some were operated only at irregular intervals.

Though the Llano Colony was established as a purely materialistic community, and made its appeal almost exclusively to those who held the materialistic view, it gradually changed, recognizing that this dogma of selfishness, while it might have a good foundation of truth and was highly logical, did not stand all of the tests of a complete truth. There grew up an ethical understanding, referred to frequently as spiritual, tho not in a religious sense, and this began to mould itself into making the principles of co-operation supply the place of the religious beliefs which gave such cohesiveness to religious communities.

This was pretty well expressed in the Declaration of Principles, which was salvaged from a rather pretentious Constitution intended to be used by the colony, but which was abandoned after several weeks of wrangling. The Declaration of Principles was intended as an outline of behavior, and its provisions were as follows:

Declaration of Principles

In conducting the affairs of the Llano del Rio Colony it has been found that the fewer inflexible rules and regulations the greater the harmony. Instead of an elaborate constitution and a set of laws the colonists have a Declaration of Principles and they live up to the spirit of them. The Declaration follows:

1. Things used productively must be owned collectively.

2. The rights of the community shall be paramount over those of any individual.

3. Liberty of action is permissible only when it does not restrict the liberty of another.

4. Law is a restriction of liberty and is just only when operating for the benefit of the community at large.

5. Values created by the community shall be vested in the community alone.

6. The individual is not justly entitled to more land than is sufficient to satisfy a reasonable desire for peace and rest. Productive land held for profit shall not be held by private ownership.

7. Talent and intelligence are gifts which should be rightly used in the service of others. The development of these by education is the gift of the community to the individual, and the exercise of greater ability entitles none to the false reward of greater possessions, but only to the joy of greater service to others.

8. Only by identifying his interests and pleasures with those of others can man find real happiness.

9. The duty of the individual to the community is to develop to the greatest degree possible by availing himself of all educational facilities and to devote the whole extent of that ability to the service of all.

10. The duty of the community to the individual is to administer justice,

to eliminate greed and selfishness, to educate all, and to aid any in time of age or misfortune.

ARMY OF INDUSTRY
1914 to Present Time

Though a small colony, and one which has receded rather than progressed, still the contribution of the Army of Industry at Auburn, California, to the experimental work of community living is worth considerably more than its numerical importance indicates.

The following excerpts from "Let's Go," a publication of the organization, put out in New York under date of May, 1924, sum up most of these experiences under the title "A Little History." The space devoted to this rather small experiment is justified because its experiences were in vest-pocket form, much the same as those of larger experiments and are vividly set forth by Mr. Geraldson:

"Up to 1914 we had a big, live Socialist Local at Auburn, California, a typical local very much like many others all over the U. S. at that time. We were constantly proselyting and constantly 'doing politics.' We bought and distributed much literature; voted on the incessant stream of referendums always coming along and dug up much money for various of the activities carried on by the 'movement' at that time.

"Out of all this activity and discussion a new idea gradually became dominant in the minds of several of us and finally came to be discussed more than any other one topic. It was that: 'If the goal of all this effort is a co-operative civilization, presumably restricted in some way as to the holding of property by individuals, the way to reach such civilization must lie in starting here and now and building it.' * * * The upshot of it all was that finally a number of the most active, energetic members of the local closed up their affairs and went to the Llano Colony, while others joined hands in establishing a smaller 'colony' on a fine fruit farm in the Sierra foothills near Auburn to give the new idea a tryout. * * *

"When we started out there were quite a number of rank-and-file Socialists among us, several members of the I. W. W., and a number of persons of various other view points—about forty in all. We did not incorporate, but threw several families and several lots of property of one sort or another together tentatively, for the use of all so far as possible, for a year, agreeing to carry the enterprise on as a unit for that time and to be guided as to our future course by what we learned. And we learned a lot.

"As was to be expected, when we got down to business, there turned out to be about as many different ideas as to how we were to do things as there were people in the group. Also, there was a great diversity of opinion as to how to do almost every item of the work we had in hand and as to who should do the various kinds of work we had to do in carrying on the orchard or 'farm.' Also, it soon developed that quite a large percentage had come with us, not for any ideal or with any sincere desire to serve, but merely to get an easy living and anything else that they could.

"We reasoned from the first that the easiest people to reach and the people most in need of the relief to be offered by co-operative activity, were those persons who had ben crowded off the Property Band Wagon, who were 'broke'; and so we made admission to our 'union' free, depending on the labor power of the members, after they were 'on the job' to keep their wants supplied and the bills paid. Those of us who were in line to contribute property of any kind to the scheme presumably felt that we could add that little to our labor power in our desire to serve the common good, without any special compensation. It was all pretty vague at first, but we kept the door open anyway to the propertyless person who sought our haven, and, of course, acquired a fine bunch of 'getters' who wasted, stole, and destroyed faster than the others could produce, to the end that we went behind several hundred dollars a month for all of that first year. We had a good crop of fruit which sold at fair prices, but we had borrowed so much for running expenses that we came out at the end of the year poorer than we went in.

"Of course, we had the typical radicals' ideas as to democracy: that each one should have a 'say' about everything concerning the group and its activities, and so on. We elected a 'supervisor' of the group and various heads of departments. We met often and 'discussed' much, even as to how any money we had on hand should be disbursed. I recall one sharp debate as to whether we should buy clothes for the children or whiskey for the men.' We appointed committees and sent them to make purchases and did everything else about after the approved fashion. It often took us until nine or ten o'clock in the morning to argue out the details of the day's work. During the winter there was much pruning of fruit trees to do, which is urgent, skilled work. Often a bonfire was built and more talking done than pruning, to the end that we got very much behind though having three times as many men on the job as a Japanese tenant would have had. No elected supervisor of the pruning could do more than coax or scold.

"At first we established a rule that each man should have five dollars Saturday night to 'go to town on.' As that was before the 'dry' regime this sum always enabled several of them to get very drunk, made a very noticeable hole in our funds, and, of course, had a very demoralizing effect in other ways, often leading to disgraceful brawls that were witnessed by women and children, as well as to other ills. Later we reduced this 'town' money to two dollars a week, but it was then used to buy alcohol and made about as much trouble as ever. To make up the shortage, fruit, chickens, and hogs were several times taken to town and sold to get money for liquor. One man took a horse and wagon for the same purpose. * * * We had valuable horses, too large for speed, ridden and driven beyond all reason; in some cases to their very definite injury, and vehicles of all kinds driven and battered to the limit.

"* * * We had 'Sociologists' who also managed to avoid work of any kind, but were always on hand at meal time. One fellow in particular, of this type, captured the entire milk supply on one occasion and hid it away so that he could have peaches and cream while the rest of us, except the children, were not even having milk. He was highly indignant when the milk was restored to the children and denounced the procedure as 'tyranny.'

"We always extended the 'glad hand' to strangers and lent a sympathetic ear to tales of woe, to the end that we were imposed on in endless ways by persons who came there out of curiosity or to 'take a rest.' * * *

"Those of us who have survived have learned more about human nature than we ever thought existed. We see humans now just as lovable animals with a good deal of hair and primal instinct left and a very thin veneer of 'civilization,' 'idealism,' 'altruism,' attached. Even those who have had 'the best opportunities' turn out to be utterly 'human' when this very thin covering is penetrated. And communal activity soon penetrates the covering. We can't pose or bluff very long, and 'get away with it' in the communal group. So some more 'very valuable' acquisitions left us to our fate.

"Here, as elsewhere, Economic Determism determines. Grocery bills, interest, taxes, and the like, shape policies and dictate methods. While these will not exist in the New Civilization, they will continue around its edges until the whole world is reorganized—that is, we shall have surpluses to sell and various things to buy. Our people were hearty eaters, wore out many shoes and much clothing, and were wasteful and expensive otherwise. Some devoted workers for the Common Good took employment on the outside and turned what they earned into the common fund, and still we went behind.

"When the end of the first year came around we had a lot of problems to think out as best we could. Were we going to continue? If so, how were we going to organize? What was going to be our policy on various questions? * * * We had been gradually curbing the liquor supply by withholding money, were again denounced as tyrants and lost a family or two of wastrels, also some single men, but we had gained some valuable recruits. As far as we could reason it out we regarded our enterprise as one composed of people who did not OWN anything individually. We had found that whenever questions of ownership arose the harmony was destroyed. * * * We who had property wanted it to be held in some way so as to benefit humanity in general, not any certain group of persons. * * *

"So we decided to continue, most of us. And we decided to continue to offer free admission to persons who would meet certain reasonable requirements, for we desired, and it seemed logical, to offer relief to persons who really needed it, not to persons who had more or less money and so, did not need it. Those of us at the 'hub' decided that, as those already in had made no 'investment,' except in a very few cases, and had been admitted free, they were in no position to question or pass on the admission of others.

"We maintained the group at the hub almost intact and they agreed that it was the logical thing to do in the light of our experience. Later we withdrew all consideration of money matters, of buying, selling, and so on, from the members, finding that these, like divided ownership, were 'Property Activity,' and all led to divided economic interests and to a divided household. We were seeking solidarity.

"So a little group of us in California, working at and thinking of nothing else for nearly ten years now, have been able to uncover economic truths of the greatest importance, just as definitely as if our numbers had been vastly greater. We did not deal with selected people; with such as could pay a given fee, or persons of culture and refinement; but with just plain, every-day humans, particularly 'losers' in the property game. Through fortuitous circumstances we were early led to either banish or lock up OWNERSHIP, which fact opened wide the door to economic understanding."

A letter received by the compiler of this volume in 1923 from a resident of the colony at Auburn sheds some additional light on the bright side of the enterprise and indicates the viewpoint of those who remained:

"We are just a little group of 'broke' people working together as one family, each one doing his or her share of the work according to ability in return for food, clothing, shelter, education, recreation, and other human rights according to available resources. Each member entering must certify that he or she is without property, must be willing to give up the idea of getting rich, and have no voice in the handling of property affairs until such time as appointed by the Director.

"During our experience of the last nine years we have not missed one meal at the common table, and during that time many have come and gone, a thousand or such matter—lawyers, doctors, university students, lumber jacks, teamsters, carpenters, and people from all walks of life—all have mingled with us as one big family.

"We have leased ten or twelve different ranches where we have raised cattle, hogs, horses, goats, rabbits, chickens, hay, vegetables, and fruit. Some of us have even gone into the slave pens at times to hire out for whatever the market offered in order to get cash for the general support of all and at the same time scatter propaganda among workers on the job.

"At first we took in those who owned property, called meetings every week-end and voted upon all property matters. This led to no end of difficulty, and finally we abandoned all tactics of a property organization and gathered about us those who were without property and willing to serve the common interest upon faith. Of course, those who owned something felt that they had a lot to lose, so they took their possessions and left, while those who had nothing remained to become loyal members of the group. Our idea is to form many groups with a leader of each appointed as a result of long experience and loyal adherence. * * *"

Gerald Geraldson writes of his enterprise from New York as follows:

Ernest S. Wooster, Leesville, La.,

Although we feel that we have accomplished social research work of the greatest importance, and that we have uncovered economic laws that must be understood and conformed with before anything in the way of real social rebuilding can be accomplished in the world at large, still we do not consider that we are in a position to claim anything very concrete or tangible, to the mind of the casual observer, in the way of actual organization work accomplished.

We started out in 1914, a very miscellaneous group of thirty or forty just average humans, who were agreed merely on the one point that we would try to work together, on as near a democratic basis as we could get, and as long as we felt so disposed. The dominant element were former "political Socialists" who had vaguely reached the conclusion that if the goal of Socialistic effort is a co-operative civilizaton, the way to reach it must be to start with such persons as are agreed and build it. We have had much proof of the soundness of this view and, as I said, have learned many things, mostly outlined in various issued of our little paper, "Let's Go!" but we have not increased in numbers—have, indeed, lost all but eight or ten. This, we believe, is because California is the easiest place in the U. S. to get along, and so the most difficult place for any movement really looking to a change to make headway.

We have, however, always managed to maintain a free "common table" and a little nucleus who are now fully agreed on the fundamentals of the problem. We believe that "fertile soil" for our "gospel" will be found, not where economic conditions are easy, but where they are hard. Therefore we are concentrating our efforts in this city, and hope before long to commence work in Europe.

As we say often in the paper, we now believe that the New Civilization will make its first tangible appearance as little groups of wage workers in the large cities, who will be forced into co-operation by rising rents and other economic pressure We have sent you some copies of the paper.

KUZBAS (Russia)
1922 to Present Time

No colony ever made a more spectacular start than Kuzbas, the Russian experiment under the Soviet government. It enlisted William D. Haywood, one of the foremost American radicals, an I. W. W. of international standing. It sent to Russia hundreds of Americans and thousands of dollars were raised by friends for the Kuzbas colonists. Workers from many countries congregated to work out on a large scale, and under what seemed remarkably favorable conditions, an experiment which promised to be successful from the first, so far as material welfare was concerned. The Russian government was friendly and gave the colonists valuable concessions.

From the St. Louis Post Despatch, in an issue in June, 1924, we take the following account.

Imagine yourself on a warm summer evening on the highest ridge of a bleak, crescent-shaped range of hills, covered with scrubby timber. You face the setting sun. From the circle of the horizon, stretching toward you from north, west and south is a vast sweep of black land, overgrown with coarse brown grass, but marked here and there with patches of green fields and the even rows of cultivated land. Mist veils the low hollows. Half a mile away a muddy river, edged with tall timber, bends around to form an oval plain. At the foot of the hills is what appears to be a large spread of pine boxes, just set about at various angles with no attempt at alignment. These are the rough unpainted frame and log houses of Kemerova.

Off to the side are reddish mounds alongside of black gaps—the coal and iron mines. Then, with the thermometer registering 30 below, imagine the same scene, a wind-swept land of snow, the boxes half buried, the roads channels of snow packed four feet deep and series of drifts like high waves over the plain, all glistening with a blinding brilliance under the winter sun—and you have a bird's-eye view of Kemerova in four months of summer and eight months of winter, as described by Mrs. Hand.

"The houses, which are nearly all alike, are built by the Soviet government for the miners and other workers," said Mrs. Hand. "They are two or three-room structures with water and electric lights. The furniture, too, plain and of the same pattern in all houses, is unfinished unless one wants to wait, in which case the government will paint it. A few buildings are larger, such as the theater (built by the American Relief Commission), a meeting house, the co-operative store, the hospital, the community eating house, and a few homes of officials. After the summer thaw, the streets are deep with mud, as in any new town where the streets are not paved.

"The population is about 2000, of which 200 are Americans, including 50 women. The remainder is made up of Russians, Lithuanians, Tartars,

Germans, and many other nationalities."

A letter from Herman Carlson, formerly a member of the Llano Co-operative Colony, who went to Kuzbas, sheds some light on the affairs of the big Kuzbas Colony. Carlson is well-known to the author, and is a man of quiet and dispassionate observation. He writes to George T. Pickett:

"As you say, the crisis is approaching rapidly. I have a certain fear of the day when the capitalist will be forced to turn over his possessions and the administration to the workers. With the experience I have had in contact with class-conscious workers who came here from America, I hardly think they are ripe yet.

"They came here to help build up Russia. The first thing some of them did as soon as they had small holes in their socks was to go on strike to get new socks; when out of tobacco the same thing happened. The only thing they remembered from America was when they had pork chops, and, according to their stories, they must have been eating a whole lot of it. Furthermore, as they remembered it, America must be a real Heaven for the toilers and the capitalists are the same as angels put there by some divine power to guard the workers that no harm is done them. But I had different experiences in America.

"The day they left America for Russia they consider their most unhappy day and the most unlucky turn in their lives. The Russians are too uncivilized to live among * * * and many of them, after a few days, went back to America and assured their associates that their radicalism was cured forever. Of course, there are many things in Russia that we do not like. There are classes seen, but they are left over from the Czar's time and are not a product of the revolution. The Soviet government is doing the best it can to iron it out.

"They have night schools for the grown-up illiterates.

"I am no longer in Kuzbas. The winter time there is too severe, and my health did not permit me to stay during the winter months * * *"

Herman Carlson's description of the radicals at Kuzbas will recall to the reader the characterization made by Mr. John A. Collins of the Skaneateles Colony, who said: "Our previous convictions have been confirmed that not all who are most eager for reform are competent to become successful agents for its accomplishment—that there is floating upon the surface of society a body of restless, disappointed, jealous, indolent spirits, disgusted with our present social system, not because it enchains the masses to poverty, ignorance, vice, and endless servitude, but because they could not render it subservient to their private ends. Experience convinces us that this class stands ready to mount every new movement that promises ease, abundance, and individual freedom * * *"

Here again we have an example of the necessity of a motivating force other than a philosophy based on pure materialism. These radicals who were

willing to go to Russia, but who had so little of the spirit of the enterprise
that they struck for socks and tobacco, were intent only on their own affairs,
and to them the Kuzbas Colony was merely a fancied opportunity to get more
for themselves. They did not wish to assist in making it a success; they wanted others to do that, but were apparently eager to profit individually in every
way possible.

It is significant that William D. Haywood, organizer and promoter of
the Kuzbas Colony, was early ousted from his position. Haywood was one
of the most belligerent of American radicals, and it was currently reported
that he slipped into Russia while out of prison on bonds, leaving his bonds-
men to pay. Haywood was an exponent of sabotage and of industrial re-
prisal, and though a strong leader and a powerful organizer and propagandist, he was lacking in the ethical and spiritual insight which seems so imperative to community success.

LESSER COMMUNITIES OF TODAY

A COLONY OF FINNS
1921 to Present Time

The Wayne Produce Association is a co-operative colony made up of
Finnish people, located at McKinnon, via Jessup, Georgia, established in
April, 1921. It is an attempt to reconcile certain phases of modern capitalism with some of the fundamentals of communism, but without complete
success, according to Mr. Isaac Ahlborg.

Its form of organization is that of a corporation, with stock issued to the members to represent their financial interests in the concern,
with a Board of Directors and a General Manager selected at semi-annual
meetings. The entrance fee is $750, and each member is allotted half an
acre of ground on use-lease, but builds his own house upon it. A peculiar
feature is that only the purchaser of the stock is a member, others of his
family not being members. This is an attempt to reconcile the inequality
of representation and expense between single men and those with families.
According to Mr. Ahlborg this is not entirely successful, for these is a strong
tendency to alienate the non-members. These are employed when there is
need for additional labor; but there is no guarantee of employment for them
as there is for others who are stock-holding members. Obviously there is
a burden placed on the man or family; for, while his income from the Colony is the same as that of the single man, his expense must be greater. To

off-set this, many must go out and seek work elsewhere, while others are put to such individualistic devices as raising poultry and growing vegetables on their building lots.

The wages system is in vogue, the daily allowance being about $2.50, of which $1 is accummulated credits to be paid in cash or equivalent when the resources of the colony permit, the remaining $1.50 to be paid in cash when current expenses have been deducted. Single men occupy rooms in the lodging house, and pay rent for them; they also pay for meals at the boarding house. Whatever remains is paid to them in cash, disbursements being made twice monthly. All are paid at the same rate, regardless of occupation.

About 75 members, some of them with families, but not all of them continuous residents of the colony, make up the Wayne Produce Association. The chief industry is truck gardening—cabbage, sweet potatoes, Irish potatoes, corn, beans, cauliflower, turnips, and beets, with other vegetables at times, being marketed in Tampa, Savannah, Jacksonville, and Chicago. Two cars of potatoes were shipped early in 1924.

The membership is recruited largely from among Communists, Industrial Workers of the World, and members of the Workers' Party, and has been restricted to Finnish people exclusively. Their common agreement is on the desirability of a practical demonstration of their convictions, and their motto indicates this: "Each for all and all for each." There is no general religious belief; probably most of them are at least non-religious, if not anti-religious, though a few profess religious convictions. Most of them were coal and iron mine workers, woodsmen, and industrial workers, and all have been residents of the United States for many years.

A protective feature of the membership requirement is that only able-bodied men between the ages of 18 and 45 be accepted for membership. The purpose is, of course, to insure that all are able to be productive workers.

About 800 acres of land have been purchased, and other land will be bought as needed, but the unexpected raise in taxes has deterred buying land in excess of present needs. The land is cut-over and the stump-puller is kept busy clearing for extending operations.

The school system is a combination of public and private school, the term being extended by the colony by advancing funds when the public appropriation has been used up. The colony in 1923 paid about 40 per cent of the salary. The building was put up by the colony.

Applications for membership are passed on by the Board of Directors, but members are permitted to come only when it is deemed that the colony is able to profitably employ more men. There is no difficulty in securing members. Good character is required, and an effort is made to secure those who have a good understanding of the principles of the organization.

142

Members who prove unworthy to remain may be sent out. Some leave for other reasons, frequently because they can prosper more outside the colony. Those wishing to dispose of their membership stock may do so, but the purchaser must be approved by the Board of Directors before being permitted to become a resident member.

The program of the colony is almost wholly agricultural. There are, in addition to the gardening, a store, hotel, blacksmith shop, dairy, poultry and sawmill. In the poultry department 800 mature hens and 2,000 baby chicks started the season of 1924, and the equipment includes a chicken house 18 x 150 feet. The dairy has 40 cows, though not all are giving milk. The colonists have 90 pigs of the Duroc-Jersey breed mostly, four mules, one horse, two tractors, one truck, and an automobile. Some butter is made, milk is furnished the colonists, and there is occasionally some for outside sale.

All business is conducted on a cash basis, including the sale of colony products. These are sold through the store at estimated cost. Meals are priced at cost at the boarding house, which is expected to accommodate only single men. Many employ themselves growing vegetables or raising poultry at home. No livestock other than poultry is permitted by individuals.

A monthly general assembly is held at which colony business is discussed, and differences of opinion many be aired. Apparently this is a successful institution in the Wayne colony. This may be due to the fact that all are Finnish people and may be able to get along together better than Americans would, or mixed nationalities might, in handling delicate and personal questions in this manner. The assembly meets once each month—the first Sunday.

The social life consists of a dance each alternate Saturday, with entertainments on the other Saturdays. No admissions are charged and outsiders are invited to attend. At the entertainments much stress is laid on the necessity of having the colony spirit.

Women are not employed generally.

Judging from the experience of other colonies, it would seem that a peculiar weakness of the Wayne colony is the system of considering only the stock-holding member of the family as a member of the colony. Another weakness is the tendency toward judging members by the product of their labor, rather than the willingness to perform.

That not all of the plans of the colony are entirely satisfactory is indicated by the desire of some of the members to study other colonies to try to learn of methods which might overcome some of the difficulties met. The spirit of individualism is to some extent encouraged by the plan of organization of the Wayne Produce Company, and to obviate this, some of the members have been contemplating a fundamental change to the family system, abolishing the wage system entirely and making all residents of the colony members of it.

HEAVEN EVERYWHERE
Established in 1923

Albert J. Moore of Chicago, president and founder of The Life Institute and publisher of many pamphlets, established a colony at Heaven City, near Harvard, Illinois in 1923, held by the Humanity Trust Estate. Its avowed purpose was to solve all of the world's ills, how to live well, to be satisfied, and to be happy. A prospectus says: "Live to live, not just to make a living. Live and have everything free; no rent to pay, no food to buy, no clothes to buy, no doctor bills to pay, no dentists to pay, no nurses to pay, no taxes (almost), no insurance to keep up, no death to worry over, no funeral expenses, no hell (like most people now have), no heaven to go to when you die, no charities to keep up, no poor relations, no schools books to buy. A place to live and to be happy, free as the air you breathe."

Moore prophesied that 1923 would be known as the year of the world's greatest money panic, that 1924 would be a year of universal labor strikes, bringing horrible devastation, and that 1925 would bring on reactionary revolution on a world-wide scale, to be followed in 1926 by a world war which would wipe out three fourths of the world's population. Following this would be the "new dawn."

Requirements are that no jewelry be worn and that members possess no private property elsewhere, such as real estate, but must dispose of it before entering the colony; no insurance is carried, taxes are paid by the trustee; instruction is free; family units are preserved; corpses are cremated; reincarnation is a part of the belief of the founders; expulsion can be only on the grounds of refusal to work and by the unanimous vote of all; all forms of recreation are encouraged; Froebel and Montessori systems in the schools.

The basis of the colony is religious. No great material advance has been possible in the short time since the colony was established, and in answer to a letter requesting some information regarding the enterprises, S. P. Talcott, trustee for the Humanity Trust Estate, writes:

"We are not in shape to make up the kind of story desirable. All the facts are contained in the enclosed booklet, Heaven Everywhere, from which you may quote as suits you, except that we have only 130 acres of land in this one section. We invite no one and give anything we have to any one desiring what we have. We consider the child first. We have cows, cars, horses, goats, and money sufficient unto our needs and the ability to get whatever we want from time to time."

HERRENHUTER BRUDER GEMEINDE
Established in 1500 (about)

This was organized by the Moravian Brothers and deserves mention here because of its singular success in an undertaking which is usually highly commercialized and rather intricate, requiring menial servility rather than equality. The Moravain Brothers are not celibates, but at one time practiced the unusual system of drawing wives by lot.

The location is very healthful, and one of the chief sources of income is conducting a health and summer resort. Adolph Schillinger, to whom we are indebted for this brief account, tells of having been in their village a number of times. He says it was noted for its cleanliness, the intelligence of the people, and their high character. Their school was so ably conducted that wealthy families sent their daughters there for a year or so for the educational advantages.

Though the colonists conduct a brewery among their enterprises, visitors are limited to two glasses of beer, indicating that sobriety is not only taught but enforced among the Moravian Brothers.

UNITED CO-OPERATIVE INDUSTRIES
Established 1923
(Account by Walter Millsap, its founder)

This is an organization that has for its central idea the equal participation in all benefits, but not equal participation in management. That statement should probably be further modified to say that there is equal opportunity to participate in all the benefits, but the actual participation is determined by several factors, the principal ones of which are the amount of time spent by the individual, the amount of money or the value of tools and equipment which he has contributed by means of which his time and the time of others is made valuable, and the ability of the individual to meet average requirements in the matter of performance.

This may sound complicated, but it is not. Space does not permit us to give the details, and the above statement can be accepted.

This plan has been in operation for over a year now. The product that we have put out has brought, in the aggregate, about $10,000.00. This has been distributed among salesmen outside of the organization, among employes within the organization as wages, and among dealers who have supplied material.

Considering all elements, no profits have as yet been realized, because expenses have been incurred, the effect of which can be realized only over a period of years.

Some of the activities, taken by themselves, have paid good profits, but instead of distributing them, they have been used to increase the capital, and this, of course, belongs to the shareholders, or those who hold shares and work also.

There is no participation in profits or in the ownership of the accumulating property except by those who are both share-holders and workers. And then this is in proportion to the amount of work and the amount of time and the efficiency of the work. A worker must accomplish as much as the average of other workers on that job or he cannot be employed. He must hold shares or his time will not be considered for profit shares and he will receive only wages. A share-holder must be a worker also to entitle him to any share in the profits or ownership in the accumulating property.

We have worked out many of the details and functions and we have satisfied ourselves that they are practical. The spirit of co-operation that has been displayed by all of our people is perfectly wonderful.

We have had little social life as yet. We had one party and dance recently that was a pronounced success, and we hope to have more of them; but until our friends can live closer together this will not be easy.

We had one unfortunate occurrence. One man who had splendid ability in a certain line became over-anxious and thought he could hasten matters by abandoning the original plan and getting the property and business which belongs to the shareholders into his own hands. He used much diplomacy, but our Trustees proved that they can think straight in a crisis, and could be trusted. This means much to all who are interested in any way in United Co-operative Industries and to those who are watching to see how this form of organization will work in the field of co-operative endeavor. Naturally we had to dismiss this man. We lost no other people except the members of his family. We lost some time and some business, but the morale of the whole organization is stronger than ever, and we know from experience that our foundations are sound.

We hope soon to try the plan of annexing other activities, carefully, of course, and one at a time. Eventually we want to get a more beautiful location, and have some land. We hope to grow until we become a self-contained and self-supporting community, but we must learn as we go, and under no circumstances allow ourselves to go faster than we learn.

Our prospects are very bright, indeed, at the present time.

INDIVIDUALISTIC "COLONIES"

The word "colony" is used so loosely, and such different meanings have been attached to it, that perhaps an account of some of the individualistic colonies might be useful to give some idea of the failures that attend enterprises which have little idealism and nothing of communal living at all.

We are again indebted to L. S. Witmer for an account of another Ruskin—not the one of communistic memory. It is one of later origin and of quite different ideas and ideals.

"Along about the year 1910," writes Mr. Witmer, "some parties bought a big body of land here to start a colony. This was to be an ideal individualistic colony. In this colony the people would rule; they would meet in mass the first Saturday of each month and make all the laws, rules, and regulations. Whatever they said went. But it was understood beforehand that this was not to be a communistic or socialistic colony as a whole.

" 'We are not among those who fear the people, said the promoters, 'so come all who want to and take a hand.' This sounded good to many people, and they came from all parts of the world * * * As soon as there were enough people on the ground to do anything, they decreed that this would be strictly a white man's settlement and that no intoxicating liquors or cigarettes should be manufactured and sold. Also that there should be schools and colleges. All of this was very good, and more people came, and among them were many learned people. Ruskin was made up almost wholly at first of well-informed and educated people.

"Land is the foundation upon which all things rest and, of course, this was the first great question that the colony had to deal with. 'Gentlemen,' said one of their number, 'this is a fine country here. The location is exceptionally fine. The land lies well and it works nicely. It is very easily drained, and much of it can be irrigated from flowing wells only 200 feet down. The climate is fine and healthful, and crops will grow the year around, and almost every grain and grass and fruit and vegetable known to the whole world to-day can be grown here. The soil is not rich, it is true, but it can be made very productive. * * * This means that this will be a very thickly-settled country some day, an empire within itself and a perfect paradise of loveliness. Land will be away up in price. The thing for us to do now is to get all we can of this land while the getting is good and the price is low.'

"The temptation was irresistible. The land speculators were soon in the majority and when a vote was taken they carried the day. An era of land speculation and grafting then set in. All on the ground bought all they could of the land, and many of them went back north to sit down and wait and get rich. They told others, who came and saw and bought and went away to sit down and wait and get rich. And on and on they came and saw and bought, until the great body of the land passed out of the hands of the big speculators, and the last state is worse than the first.

"If we want to do anything with this land now, we have thousands of people to deal with, scattered here and there all over the U. S. or the world —and that is a job.

"Ruskin was to be an ideal community, a little paradise or heaven here on earth. * * * But no sooner had these people come together to do their work than that old serpent or devil 'get-something-for-nothing' appeared. But the devil did not look to the people of Ruskin like they thought he would when they came to kill him. He didn't have those long horns and that forked tail as he had always been pictured. He was a pretty good-looking fellow after all. He looked an angel, a perfect angel of light.

"'What is wrong with buying 20, 40, or 80 acres of this land now for a few dollars and then selling it in a few years at a big price?' This is what these people asked themselves. * * * Ruskin became like any other place where both good and evil would be done * * * There sorrows and troubles were greatly multiplied until many of them could endure it no longer and returned from whence they came.

"The day they voted to let everybody in Ruskin have land to do as was pleased by the holders, they killed every ideal."

Mr. Witmer was in both Ruskin and Topolobampo. Both failed. One was communistic, one was individualistic. One wanted to rid the community of profits, the other made the profit-making system a part of its life. Mr. Witmer has much of praise for Topolobampo with all of its crudities and mistakes, for at least there was a high purpose and genuine sacrifices for a principle, whereas in this individualistic Ruskin there was only a scramble for profits, and this scramble shook loose the rather insecure ideals which some had brought in with them.

* * * * *

The other individualistic colony which comes to us as a direct contrast is the LaGloria Colony of Cuba. We are indebted to Arthur Greenwood of La Gloria for the information. As a contrast with the Cosme Colony of Paraguay, it shows the difference between the idealism that withstands hardships for a principle and the individualism that withstands hardships but goes out in search of profits.

"Ernest S. Wooster:

* * * Now to your inquiry: This so-called 'colony' was started some 20 years ago as the La Gloria Land and Steamship Company, to start a grape-fruit to be the specialt es. There had been 200,000 acres acquired grape fruit to be the specialties. There have been 200,000 acres acquired with this in view. The land sold in 5, 10, 15, and 20-acre tracts, at first at $10 an acre; but at the height of the boom favored locations sold as high

148

as $100 an acre. Many folks, led by glowing accounts of a life in the semi-tropics, raising oranges at good profits, came here. We had at one time about 2000 colonists and great activity in the clearing and planting of groves. Those were pleasant and invigorating days when all were roughing it. Finally the trees began to bear beautifully and shipments began. Then we discovered that the slow and poor transportation and the sharp practices of the commission men in the entry ports of New York and New Orleans, etc., left no returns for the fruit. But still we persisted with grape fruit later, and when we had begun to get occasional returns the U. S. put a tariff of 85 cents a box on all.

"From that time on we began to dwindle, and many sold out at a sacrifice and new-comers ceased to arrive. Later, when our fruit was lying under the trees rotting, the despised Cuban came around and offered a few dollars a thousand for the oranges.

"Now there is a new movement. The abandoned land is being taken up for the planting of sugar cane. There has also come a railroad line thru the valley some four miles from town, and large areas of the land are being leased to a company * * * for 15 years. They pay a sliding scale of profits on the yield of cane based on the market price of cane for the year. I turned my 15 acres over to them last year and it has been planted one year * * * The returns for several years have averaged $40 to $50 an acre. I am making arrangements to sell my goods and house in town and seek another home.

"Later the Cuban market developed for oranges and those who did not abandon their groves, but kept them up, now can get a fair return from them. But they are few and mostly old folks.

"Now as to the community: In the early days the social life here was delightful; but when the slump came it brought out all of the greed, selfishness, and duplicity, and for years the place has been a gossipy, back-biting and swindling bye-word. We had two churches—Methodist South Church and Episcopalian—and even at our best they seemed to be always bickering and striving for the town's social and financial lead. For a long time now neither has had any pastor—too poor to pay for one. * * * It has been absolutely impossible to inculcate any co-operative ideas into this 'colony.' Selfishness and suspicion being so deeply and terribly seated. Nothing ever held them together, not even impending failure. There are perhaps one hundred 'whites' left."

Communal colonization plans are not the only ones which fail. Here was a colony with great potential wealth. It failed. While the causes of failure were obvious enough, yet the causes of many of the communal colonies' failures were also obvious and were not due to the form of organization, but to other circumstances, often of a material nature and quite outside the communities.

ANALYSIS OF COMMUNITY ENTERPRISES

The purpose of this little volume would not be completely served were there no effort made to summarize and analyze the information contained.

A comparison of Communities shows that, tho the conditions were much the same, taking all things into consideration, yet the religious colonies showed much better results. Possibly this is due in no small measure to the fact that they nearly always had strong leaders during the critical years of the formative period, the time when the habits of community life and the traditions were being set. The affairs of the community were directed without question by the leaders, who were strong and capable; while the members devoted themselves to the manual labor of the enterprise without question. No time was lost in general assembly law-making. Their industry brought them success and prosperity.

While this system of childish and implicit trust in leaders might be questioned, and is surely open to serious doubts as a general policy, yet the leaders who embarked on such precarious enterprises as community-making were necessarily honest and earnest men and women, and the affairs of the colonists were safe in their hands. Perhaps there have also been many attempts of which we know nothing, attempts made by men incapable of conducting the affairs and solving the problems which confronted them.

Probably the success of the religious colonies has been due to the fact that their community affairs have always been a means to an end which they considered of infinitely more importance. They were not living for the community; it was merely an economical and convenient method of establishing the religion which was so vital to them. The patriarchal leader stood in the same relationship to them as did the patriarchs of old. Their obedience to their spiritual leader was implicit, and he directed their worldly affairs in the same way. Whatever quarrels they had could readily be adjusted by the leader in which they placed such supreme faith. Their community was not a demonstration of earthly affairs; it was a place in which they lived while preparing for a life beyond, and it was of less importance to them than was the Heaven for which they were preparing.

But in the secular or economic colonies, quite a different set of ideals existed. The attention of all was focussed on the matter of making a material success. It was a business enterprise in which all were partners, all desirous of frequently exercising all the rights and privileges conferred on them as members, jealous of these rights and privileges, and fearful that they might fail to make the most of their opportunities to use them. As a business enterprise it must be conducted to secure results of a material nature. They proclaimed equal rights because they believed in them, but perhaps their belief was based to some extent on an inferiority complex. They feared domination; possibly their lives had been overshadowed by others for many years. Their desire to share alike was the protection which they, each of them, placed over themselves; but it grew less from a desire to protect the rights of others than to protect their own rights. The fanaticism with which they protected their equality and exercised it, was their desire to prevent the loss of these rights; it was also the egotism of the members expressing itself, perhaps. Equality can be expressed only thru a general assembly, for under no other conditions is this sort of equality possible. This accounts for the almost universal appearance of the general assembly in secular colonies.

This desire for equality in everything is a cry for justice, but is also implies mutual suspicion of motives, and also an envy of power. In the practice of the secular colonists, there has been so little of the ethical and of the spiritual, and so much of the material, that much of the efficiency so earnestly sought has been made impossible, and the material gains so desired have been lost. They have defeated the purpose of their organizations thru the very methods they have used to insure it. They have deified democracy and sacrificed everything to it. Being so largely materialistic and so essentially interested in the fruits of their enterprise, they have quarreled constantly over the division of these fruits. Having repudiated God, as so many have done, they have worshipped material benefits with a fanaticism that has blinded them to the shortcomings of their theories. Much of their philosophy has been that of organized selfishness.

The General Assembly which has been expected to preserve the equality and rights of members has become in many instances the chief means of destroying the prosperity of the group and consequently the rights of the members. These secular colonies have been organized selfishness; what they have been unable to get by individual effort they have banded together to get by collective effort and to divide equally, for this is, of course, the only division to which they would consent. But the inherent selfishness of the scheme has brought mutual suspicion. The General Assembly has been a device to keep everything in the open, but this has also brot into the open the suspicions harbored by each, and the evil-thinking has been propagated to corrupt others and to keep all of the members uneasy and suspicious and distrustful.

The ideals of the secular colonies have been much more clearly stated than have those of the religious colonies, but they have been intellectual concepts rather than motives; they have been reasons growing out of the desire to profit as individuals rather than to advance the principles which they claim to espouse. They have not been dishonest in this, but they have tried to arrange a system which would permit selfishness to operate as a mainspring. The effect and result has been quite the contrary.

CONCLUSION

From the history of communities given, and from the keen observations of those competent to observe and to judge correctly, what are we to conclude as regards Communities?

From a careful study of them we note that the most successful have been founded by men of strong convictions and powerful personalities. They have usually dominated until the colonies were well established and the habits formed. Some of them exacted unquestioning obedience.

There is not sufficient evidence, however, to believe that only religious colonies can succeed, for their success has depended too largely on the efforts of strong leaders. Under like conditions, perhaps secular colonies might have made a stronger showing.

But there is plenty of evidence to support the assertion that the colony which is purely economic in its ideals is not likely to succeed.

Most of those which have been successful to the greatest degree have been religious. Their creeds have differed, but they have all been strong adherents of some belief which welded them together, and their community life had been a means to an end, rather than an end in itself.

When we seek for causes for failure, we find that the secular colonies have in most cases been short-lived. Perhaps this has been because there was not a dominating personality to hold them in check and to instil virtues and insist on the forming of habits and the settling of traditions. Perhaps, tho, it was because the motive was one which disintegrates rather than integrates power and strength.

Many have had the General Assembly as a supreme power. This means that all members were expected to be able to pass judgment on important matters, regardless of their previous training or knowledge of the subject or general capability. Passions were unleashed, as they were certain to be, and in such gatherings were born the dissensions which eventually wrecked them. While history does not in all cases record this, we are justified in concluding this is true from the facts which are furnished us, and by the experiences of societies—co-operative societies especially—where such methods have been tried.

The General Assembly is a medley of opinions and bias and feeling, and, at times, of other and worse things, for hatreds grow and thrive where the General Assembly inflames passions. Into such a cauldron is thrust important legislation, delicate matters which demand the utmost coolness and calmness and the most careful consideration. It is preposterous to expect that a large group of untrained people can give heedful and unimpassioned thought to matters which are likely to be beyond their experience and which may appeal strongly to their prejudices. To entrust the management of anything so complicated and delicate as a Community into the hands of untried and hot-headed law-makers who are likely to be violently partisan and who can scarcely be hoped to be qualified, seems to be to invite failure from the very first. The history of colonies which have used this method seem to bear out this deduction.

But it is not altogether the General Assembly which makes failure come to the non-religious Communities.

It is quite as likely, more likely perhaps, to be the lack of a cohesive central thought. There is lacking that spirituality which keeps courage and faith high in the religious groups. Intent on the intricacies of colony life, a selfishness of which many were in total ignorance begins to assert itself, and this is the secret of much of the trouble which overwhelms those who become members of this fascinating form of Society.

Selfishness which seeks for personal advantages, selfishness which seeks personal aggrandizement, selfishness which seeks for superior position—these are the chief causes, and the elimination of all other causes of failure will not be sufficient if selfishness is allowed to remain.

The General Assembly is the fertile field in which Selfishness may operate, and to that extent the so-called "Democracy" of the General Assembly is a dangerous weapon placed in the hands of short-sighted and self-centered persons.

There are many contributing causes of failure. Lack of care in the examination of candidates for membership is a very important one. Half-baked idealists, impractical visionaries, persons seeking an easy life, those who have become super-annuated, those who are unwilling to accept the hard conditions which may become necessary during the pioneering period—these are a few of the unfit persons who must be guarded against.

Some colonies have failed because of poor location, but probably fewer from this reason than from any other cause. The human animal is able to get along under fearful handicaps, and if this were the only obstacle, it is probable that success would have been obtained in most cases. Most of those colonies which have lasted but a short time have been made up of people brought together hastily, an ill-assorted group with but little idea of what was necessary and with ideals which did not rise much above mere hope of personal advantage. The complexities of community life soon overwhelmed them. Few persons who have not had the experience of it can conceive of the delicate adjustments which must be made and the many perplexing problems which arise. A strong character can cope with them and can learn what way is best; weak ones are submerged by the problems which beset them and before a strong character arises the colony has gone to pieces. Integration and disintegration form a constant process with most communities, whether capitalistic or such as has been discussed here.

A successful non-religious colony must be one which substitutes a religious zeal toward its principles and an intelligent purpose of eliminating personal selfishness. Its members must observe these things with as much zeal and enthusiasm as does the colonist who believes in a life hereafter or who follows a religious leader. The principles and ideals must be transformed into what must be regarded as a religion and reverenced with as much devoutness. Those who enter a colony with other thots and with any other attitude are not likely to remain unless greatly changed within the first few months.

Materialists, wedded to their dogmas with no less firmness than are religious people, are likely to contend vigorously that certain intellectual concepts only are necessary for success in a Community, and they hold to this theory with the tenacity common to those who rely on theories.

One of the theories most prevalent has been that democracy, perfect honesty, and a scientific attitude, with complete open-mindedness, would be a suffcient basis upon which to establish a colony which would succeed because its members would not be tied to dogmas and would quickly profit by mistakes and adapt themselves to changing conditions and fuller knowledge.

Yet there is abundant material to contradict this theory, for theory it is, and not supported by facts.

Most of the secular colonies have reveled in democracy. Their history has been the story of a perfect orgy of democracy, with the whole Community occupied with every detail of management, and nothing permitted without full Community vote. The result has been almost uniformly disastrous.

But there have been colonies which have been free from dogmas, which have not been tied to Marxian theories, and which have been made up of people with unusual scientific attainments and presumably with the scientific and open-minded attitude which is so favored. Robert Owen's New Harmony had a brilliant gathering of such persons. It was not bound by Marxian philosophy, for it preceded Marx by a score of years. It was not dominated by a powerful personality, for Owen was not able to be present. It was a perfect example of the conditions which some contend so certainly are alone necessary for success. It lasted only two years, yet it was richly endowed and had everything necessary for material success. There was lacking that ethical or spiritual quality which is considered necessary by those who have given concentrated thot and whose opportunities for observation have been exceptionally good.

The Harmony Community of the Rappites is another illustration which is worth considering. Unfortunately, the chapter devoted in this book to Harmony does not do it full justice. After it was already in print, the writer got into communication with Mr. John Duss, final administrator of the affairs of the Rappites, and secured valuable new material. Mr. Duss's account of Community life among the Rappites shows that they were not tied to a religion, but that most of them were religious. Some, however, were opposed

to religion. The elder Rapp was their leader, but Frederick Rapp was looked upon with almost equal favor. Yet, after the death of both of these
the Community continued, finally rounding out a century. The cohesive
factor was a high degree of ethical conduct and a love for humanity. It did
not depend on intellectual concepts, but held toward all a genuine love and
helpfulness. Are we not justified in believing that it was this unselfishness
that had much to do with the longevity of the community? It was not founded absolutely on religion, tho generally so classified, and it had most of the
ideals and all of the material conditions which were present in the Owenite
Community at New Harmony. It gave much attention to educating its people and it had many illustrious members. The essential difference was unquestionably the spiritual quality.

Let us consider one more instance. The Llano Colony started with certain intellectual concepts. It believed in Democracy as exemplified in the
General Assembly. The members, while perhaps biased and opinionated, and
possessed of dogmatic beliefs, were, nevertheless proved to be quite flexible.
They changed their ideas to the extent of making several changes in the
form of government, trying several forms. This may not have been done
in a systematic manner, but it was nevertheless done. They blundered, but
they moved. They have been experimentalists, not scientific, perhaps, but
willing to try new ways. They have changed their methods, though they
have remained true to their original principles and ideals.

The history of the Llano Colony is the history of a change of attitude,
one from pure materialism toward one of unselfish devotion to the good of the
Community and the benefit of humanity. They have gradually introduced more
and more of the unselfishness which becomes the cohesive quality necessary
to success. It is true, perhaps, that this is still far from ideal; yet the essential thing is that they are abandoning the cold, hard intellectual concepts
which first brought them together, and are recognizing in increasing degree
the necessity of a spiritual attitude in addition to the honesty, scientific attitude, and open-mindedness which so many seem to think all-sufficient.

The history of Communities shows that the essence of success lies in the
motivating force which dominates those who go into Communities and which
will urge them in the shaping of their affairs. The directing force can take it
along the road toward success, or force it along the route to failure and
disintegration; but this will be due to the motives within the colonists.

Nothing can be clearer to those who study carefully and weigh facts than
that there is an essential motive which does not arise in the intellect, but is
more difficult to analyze and classify. Those who adhere blindly to theories
which have been repeatedly tried and proven unsuccessful, and who turn their
backs on the facts which have been so vividly brot out by the experience
of others, do not take the scientific attitude of open-mindedness which is

one of the qualifications to success in Community life, but start from the first on the dismal trail which others have followed to failure.

Embracing an ideal of unselfishness and love for humanity instead of mere special and individual benefits does not imply, as these adherents of the intellectual concept idea seem to think, that good business methods cannot be followed. The Rappites did an extensive business over wide areas of territory and were highly successful. Nor does it mean that they espouse a mushy philosophy of sentimental prayer-making. They, in fact, remain creedless but flexible, business-like, energetic, and in the main harmonious.

There must be a happy medium, a blending of the plans and purposes of the economic with the faith and enthusiasm and zeal and dogged persistence of the religious colonies. There must be freedom from dogmatic creeds, whether religion or otherwise, but there must also be the energy and fervent desire which has been so characteristic of the religious colonies. For the latter have overcome greater obstacles and have made their success in most cases thru greater privations than discouraged the economic groups.

With the driving force and cohesiveness of a religious enthusiasm and the clear-mindedness and individual initiative of the economic plans co-ordinated, there is strong reason to believe that a Community can not only exist, but can grow and thrive and prosper, expanding with the years to become a vital force in modern civilization.

CO-OPERATION AND HUMAN NATURE
By G. J. Holyoake

(From the Co-operative Classic, "History of the Rochdale Pioneers")

The moral miracle performed by our co-operators at Rochdale is that they had the good sense to differ without disagreeing; to dissent with each other without separating; to hate at times, and yet always to hold together.

In most working-class societies, and, indeed, in most public societies of all classes, a number of curious persons are found who appear born under a disagreeable star. They breathe hostility, distrust, and dissension. Their tones are always harsh. It is no fault of theirs; they do not mean it; they cannot help it. Their organs of speech are cracked and no melodious sound can come out; their native note is a moral squeak. They are never cordial and never satisfied. The restless convolutions of their skin denote a "difference of opinion"; their very lips hang in the form of a "carp"; the muscles of their faces are "drawn up" in the shape of an amendment, and their wrinkled brows frown with an "entirely new principle of action." They are a species of social porcupine whose quills eternally stick out. Their vision is inverted; they see everything upside down. They place every subject in water to inspect it, where the straightest rod appears hopelessly bent. They know that every word has two meanings, and they always take the one you do not intend. They know that no statement can include everything, and they always fix upon whatever you omit and ignore whatever you assert.

These people join a society ostensibly to co-operate with it, but really to do nothing but criticise it, without attempting patiently to improve that of which they complain. Instead of seeking strength to use it in mutual defense, they look for weakness to expose it to the common enemy. They make every associate sensible of perpetual dissatisfaction until membership with them becomes a penal infliction and you feel that you are more sure of peace and respect among your opponents than among your friends. They predict to everybody that the thing must fall—until they make it impossible that it can succeed—and then take credit for their treacherous foresight and ask your gratitude and respect for the very thing that hampered you.

Whoever joins a co-operative society ought to be made aware of this curious species of colleague whom we have described. You can get on with them very well if they do not take you by surprise. Indeed, they are useful in their way; they are the dead weights with which the social architect tries the strength of his new building. We mention them because they existed in Rochdale, and that fact serves to show that the pioneer co-operators enjoyed no favor from nature or accident. They tried like other men, and had to combat the ordinary human difficulties.